PATHWAYS
TO
PRESENCE

Making room for the presence
of God in the everyday

PATRICK WILLIS

presenceofgodhome.com

Cover art by David Cowell.

ISBN: 9798698704867

Please note the text is written in UK English which has minor spelling variations from US English (such as word endings -our/-or and -ise/-ize).

CONTENTS

PRACTICAL EXERCISES

Foreword

Christians often talk about living in the light of God's presence, but working out what that might amount to in the sometimes troubled, and always complicated, circumstances of life today can be easier said than done. What does it actually mean to experience God's presence, and how might we recognise it when we see it? What does it look like, feel like – indeed, is it supposed to be a feeling at all, or is it meant to be more a collection of beliefs? What are we supposed to actually do in order to know God's presence? Is there some technique that makes it all come alive, and if so, what might that be? And how is a life of devotion to God going to make a difference, whether for ourselves or for the communities of which we are all a part?

I hear questions like this on a regular basis – and not only from people who know that they are Christians. There are many others who are spiritually searching and find the person of Jesus in particular deeply attractive, and are desperate to find some way in which they can encounter the Christian tradition in ways that might somehow make a difference to daily living.

These and similar questions are the inspiration for this small book, with its many suggestions on meaningful spiritual practices. Some of them are ancient, reflecting lessons learned by our forebears, while others are of more recent origin and speak to the specific challenges of today's culture. They are realistic about the struggles of tough times as well as the joy of happy times. Some will appeal to you more than others, because they also reflect the diversity of the human personality and experience. But above all, the concepts presented here are more than just ideas to think about – in fact if that's all you do you'll have missed the point, so work through slowly and intentionally, taking time to discover new dimensions to skills that you already have as well as practices that may be new to you.

Back in the 17th century a Carmelite friar known as Brother Lawrence spoke of The Practice of the Presence of God, and in this book Patrick Willis invites readers to explore what that practice might now look like in the very different world of the 21st century.

John Drane – October 2020

CHAPTER 1

Seek and you will find

In my youth, I was very much a spiritual "seeker", recognising there was something in the universe bigger than me and keen to find out what it was. Across a breadth of spiritual literature, I included the Bible in my reading and found that Jesus was quoted as saying "*seek and you will find*". I felt compelled to "find" whatever it was that Jesus was offering. Exploring what that meant led me to the Christian faith.

Developing in my new-found faith I discovered other promises of Jesus, some of which seemed to jar with my experience: I read that the weary and burdened could go to him for rest and that the truth would set me free. Like many of us I felt the pull of obligation: the "should", "ought", "must" and "try" bandwagon of expectations that can come from faith, from parents, from the workplace, or simply what we expect of ourselves. I did not feel free or rested, and ironically the guilt of feeling weary and burdened just made me feel... wearier and more burdened. I also seemed to carry a vague sense of unease, as if a piece were missing, even though the teachings of my faith were clear that I should have everything I needed and I was the child of a God of peace.

Hence we come to the "why" of this book: over the years I have recognised that conscious awareness of the presence of God can help us find an authentic ease and grace in living, and experience the freedom and wholeness Jesus desires for us. We have set down the unnecessary mental baggage and found genuine refreshing and rest in God's presence.

You may already be a committed follower of Jesus, or you may be a person interested in spiritual things who is still looking for answers; in either case my sincere desire is that within these pages you will discover clearer pathways into the divine presence.

GOD'S PRESENCE IS THE KEY

The answer is close, yet we so easily miss it by turning our eyes on our problems rather than inviting in his presence. Psalm 84 gives us glimpses of how good it is living where God lives:

"How lovely is your dwelling place, Lord Almighty!".

"Blessed are those who dwell in your house; they are ever praising you."

"Better is one day in your courts than a thousand elsewhere;" [1]

So where can we find God's dwelling place, his house, his courts? The imagery and beauty described seems to put this beyond a physical temple with which the writers of the Psalm would be familiar. Many commentators point to this being a future heaven but I think there's more: the Psalmist encourages us to

---

[1] Psalm 84:1,4,10

consider those living in God's house now, not those who will live there; he points to a day in time, not a future eternity. My question is therefore: Why not us? Why not today?

If one day where God lives is better than a thousand somewhere else, that surely must be worth seeking. Perhaps on a philosophical level God is everywhere, he is *omnipresent*, but on a personal level both scripture and Christian experience recognise the practical reality of God being actively present in a *specific* way in certain places and times with certain people. Could these be the courts of the Lord that are more than a thousand times better than other places? The question therefore becomes: what are these places and times and how do we find them? Or perhaps more simply – where and how do we meaningfully meet with God?

Pete Greig, the founder of the 24x7 prayer movement describes it as:

> *"making the effort to be consciously present to the God who is constantly present to us."*

Brother Lawrence, the 17th century monastic called it:

> *"Practising the presence of God"*

In this book we will explore pathways into the presence of God. In many cases this will be taking roadblocks of our own making from the pathway, so it is clear for us to use.

There is a worship song with the words: "*in your presence all my problems disappear*" [2]. You may feel this sounds a little trite, but I believe it is true. This does not mean that life is without pain and difficulties, but we see them from a completely fresh perspective. If you make room for God's presence then everything

---

[2] Jesus, we celebrate your victory. © 1987 Thankyou Music

flows from that – deep-seated joy and peace, a sense of wholeness, genuine freedom. With these, the follower of Jesus is released into powerful service where he or she is not their own worst enemy.

Jesus says *"I stand at the door and knock";* we will look at ways to open the door, keep it open, and invite him in for dinner. Jesus also mentions that the Father and Son want to make their home with us; we will look at ways to make ourselves a welcoming place.

FOUNDATIONS AND PATHWAYS

There are two foundational themes covered in the book that are designed to help us unlock the door for Jesus: **Unconditional Acceptance** and **Intentional Attention**. Both are opportunities that sit in front of each of us right now: our choice of where and how to direct our attention, and our choice of how to respond to what we find. I think of them as spiritual life-skills that each of us will benefit from developing; they are not the purview of the extra-holy minority, they are not out of reach, they do not need special training.

On first reading, the idea of unconditional acceptance might sound weak and directionless, but it is entirely the opposite. Acceptance is spiritually powerful, and practised effectively, removes our unhelpful expectations – both of ourselves and of God, and paves the way for courageous action.

Few of us have been taught about how to intentionally manage our attention. It is most often taught in a therapeutic setting to help manage psychological issues after they have arisen, and yet consistent intentionality on where our attention is directed is a valuable life-skill for everyone – both practically and spiritually. As anyone who has trained a puppy will tell you, it can be a battle stopping it from running in circles, chewing things and making noise. Unfortunately, our minds can be just like a puppy, running in meaningless circles. The good news is they can be trained. A significant motivation for me researching and writing this book is my own puppy mind – I can still remember clearly when many years ago I was sitting in the front row of a training seminar and about five minutes in, being asked by the trainer what the three points were that he'd just outlined. I had no idea… my head had been off exploring some random fantasy of my own making. The challenge was embarrassing but effective – thirty years later I still remember it.

Intentional attention may be called mindfulness. I chose not to start with this language, as it is a word that for many people carries a set of assumptions – some positive, some negative. I wanted the reader to approach the topic with a fresh mindset, hence "intentional attention".

Having outlined attention and acceptance the book then explores five pathways into God's presence. These different pathways build extensively on the foundations of acceptance and attention so there is value in understanding these themes first.

There is nothing mystical about there being five pathways, it is merely my way to structure the book. There are doubtless other pathways I have not explored, and the pathways here are not disconnected routes but overlap multiple times. We look at slowing it down to stillness, recognising the present moment, understanding the importance of place, knowing when to praise and lament and we finally touch lightly on the most important conversations you will ever have: prayer.

Learning any new skill, it is helpful to break it down into small steps that can be practised separately, which is what I have attempted to do here by dividing up the practices into pathways. When you become fluent in them then they will flow together seamlessly.

TWO OBJECTIVES

I have two objectives designed to work together to make this book useful for you. Firstly to give you confidence that embracing God's presence more intentionally through the practices I describe is not something I made up, but is consistently confirmed by the ancient texts of Christian scripture; and secondly, to make these practices completely accessible so you can grow in your application of them without feeling lost or overwhelmed. Practice is the core purpose of this book, for without it, you have merely gained more talents without turning them into something fruitful. Jesus makes clear to us that *"from the one who has been entrusted with much, much more will be asked"* [3], hence there is wisdom in turning knowledge into lifestyle rather than simply adding to the length of your bookshelf.

-----

[3] Luke 12:48

Accessibility is at the heart of why I chose to write something new in this field. The available body of literature is not a natural source of reading material for many Christians, especially those regarding themselves as evangelical. There is less written on this crucially important topic than many, and that which has been written is frequently dense, heavy reading, which although containing practical advice, makes it easy to miss, being buried in personal mysticism with a strong dose of religious tradition. The practices described can be perceived as specialist activities for monks or the super-committed, rather than part of the lifestyle of anyone following Jesus.

There are also a new generation of books emerging covering Christian Mindfulness. These cover many of the same practices that I explore, but I wanted to start from a scriptural basis with a focus on God, rather than a focus on mindfulness. There is always a danger of making any particular practice an idol that can distract us from God rather than bring us closer.

Because of these two objectives, each pathway is handled in two parts: first there's the exploration section, where we look together at the parameters of the subject and seek to bring scriptural light; and then there's the practical section, a series of exercises to directly apply the learning from exploration. The practical sections are not normative, every practice I describe could be approached in a variety of different ways and we do well to hold specific practices lightly, being always open to new approaches. Each section also contains discussion questions to aid your personal study or to use with a small group.

Just to clear up a common question at the outset: you do not need to be a card-carrying Christian of a particular denomination to benefit from this book, but do be aware that I quote *a lot* from the Bible, the Christian scripture that many recognise as the word of God. I have used it as a prime source of authority for most of my teaching points and have sought to maintain a focus on plain, unambiguous meanings without resorting to technical examinations of obscure Greek and Hebrew texts. This would only be a distraction from getting on and doing something useful with the material.

Finally, please don't rush through the book. You may find Part 2 on the pathways easier reading than Part 1 on digging deep – it is often the case when building foundations that it feels heavy work and progress seems slow. But it is worth it! I have chosen not to pad this out with lots of stories and personal experience – you will find some of "me" in the book, but I want it to be about "you": to allow you to find your own unique way into a deepening spirituality and relationship with the divine, unhindered by unnecessary expectations or promises. And since modern-day Christians are for the most part unfamiliar with meditative and contemplative practices, you will most likely encounter ideas that will take time to process and reflect upon. You may find things you disagree with which need further study. You may be pushed out of your comfort zone – in fact I hope you are.

I wish you all the best now as you explore pathways into his presence.

PART 1

DIGGING DEEP

Where we dig the foundations of unconditional acceptance and intentional attention and warm up our spiritual muscles with some introductory exercises.

CHAPTER 2

Resistance is futile

I n continuing to teach on pathways to presence, the concept of managing inner resistance to our life situations has moved closer and closer to the beginning of my explanations as I've grasped its importance. I have now realised that a lack of acceptance, resisting your current circumstances, leads to continual blockages for those seeking to make room for God's presence. It is that important.

I have chosen the phrase *unconditional* acceptance because dropping the conditions is often the part we find the hardest. It comes across multiple times in Jesus' teachings and the writings of the apostle Paul in the Bible, sometimes hiding in plain sight. For most of us it is a profound shift in the way we view our circumstances and when you see the shift, it also releases a huge burden of expectation that we put on ourselves, and frequently transfer to God.

Instead of "acceptance", some prefer the term "surrender", it can also be thought of as "welcoming". The exact terminology is not important, the application is. As you start reading, it may feel a little like a fatalistic, "what will be, will be", but nothing is further from the truth. It is a root of strength and focus.

WHAT'S THE SECRET PAUL?

Let's start by looking at some words written by the apostle Paul in the New Testament:

> *I have learned to be content whatever the circumstances. I know what it is to be in need, and I know what it is to have plenty. I have learned the secret of being content in any and every situation, whether well fed or hungry, whether living in plenty or in want. I can do all this through him who gives me strength.*[4]

Here is the core message – "content whatever the circumstances". Paul explains further the types of situation he is thinking of: ANY situation and EVERY situation, whether he has plenty, or not enough.

Most people by this point are already panicking that this is already too lofty a goal, but Paul mentions that there was a secret to be learned, and he refers twice to a learning process, so we should expect this to take some insight and some practice. The end of this excerpt gives us a clue on Paul's secret: It is "through him who gives me strength" – the Lord Jesus Christ.

So, what is this contentment? Very simply it is embracing the present situation for what it is without any resistance. Welcoming everything, without pushing anything away. Being open to your current circumstances, whatever it may be. The reason is simple: if we spend our time resisting, we likely miss what God is doing and the opportunity to engage with him in it.

---

[4] Philippians 4:11b-13

It is so easy to find what's "wrong" with what is currently happening. Even in relatively good situations there is often something we would change; the grass is always greener, isn't it? Now especially if the situation is more difficult – for example when someone we love is ill, or we have lost a job, we can invest a lot of mental time wishing it were otherwise. It is very easy to get wrapped up in how we got here and why things are the way they are and what we don't like about it – this thinking spiral does not draw us closer to God.

SITUATIONS WE WOULD NOT CHOOSE

In life, many of us have been forced into situations we would not choose. So how will we respond: Resist the situation – or accept what is right now and make room for God in it?

Staying in Paul's letters, there is a particular example that might shock you if you really stop and think about it. In the letter it seems like a small aside as an example in a discussion about married life:

> *Nevertheless, each person should live as a believer in whatever situation the Lord has assigned to them, just as God has called them. This is the rule I lay down in all the churches. Was a man already circumcised when he was called? He should not become uncircumcised. Was a man uncircumcised when he was called? He should not be circumcised. Circumcision is nothing and uncircumcision is nothing. Keeping God's commands is what counts. Each person should remain in the situation they were in when God called them. Were you a slave when you were*

called? Don't let it trouble you—although if you can gain
your freedom, do so. [5]

The theme is not being concerned about your life situation, and then the last verse, one little verse, dropped in at the end, almost sounds trite: *If you're a slave, don't let it trouble you.* Let us pause and think about this: being a slave was in most cases a terrible existence. A slave was property – "a living tool" as one Roman author described them. You had zero rights, and your very life depended on the whim of your master. You could be treated reasonably well, you could be treated badly, and be able to do nothing about it.

Maybe you would be thinking: how can I be an effective Christian like this? What's the point of my life? Is this really God's will for me? And yet Paul says to accept the situation, don't let it trouble you. If you get opportunity to change it, absolutely go for it, but for today, fully accept the situation for what it is, and make room for God exactly where you are. In the Colossian letter, Paul also gives this encouragement to slaves.

Slaves, obey your earthly masters in everything; and do it,
not only when their eye is on you and to curry their favour,
but with sincerity of heart and reverence for the Lord.
Whatever you do, work at it with all your heart, as
working for the Lord, not for human masters [6]

In Christian teaching this verse is often re-cast to think of workplaces and the employer–employee relationship. That can be helpful, but let's not forget that this was written originally to slaves in the context of an oppressive social system. Even in this situation, scripture encourages us to embrace it fully and invite

---

[5] 1 Corinthians 7:17-21
[6] Colossians 3:22-23

God into it. Is God calling you to bloom where you have been planted rather than worrying about being somewhere else?

THE SITUATION IS NOT THE PROBLEM

Recognising that the underlying issue is not the situation itself, but how we respond, the ancient Greek thinker Epictetus expressed it well in the words: *Men are disturbed not by things, but by the view which they take of them.*

This runs contrary to common human tendency to resist and complain, to compare and to judge. The choice is ours: What view will we take? How will we respond? Back in Paul's letter to the Philippians, he offers this encouragement:

> *Do everything without grumbling or arguing, so that you may be blameless and pure, children of God without fault.*[7]

As children of God, we are invited to remain blameless by not grumbling or complaining, by not resisting the situation. When you find yourself in a situation which may be challenging to accept, complaining is a common symptom. So catching yourself complaining, either out loud or in your head, is a great way of noticing where you are not accepting of the situation and bringing the opportunity to change.

GO THE EXTRA MILE

Back in the Sermon on the Mount, among several examples of radical acceptance Jesus says this:

---

[7] Philippians 2:13

If anyone forces you to go one mile, go with them two miles. [8]

This is commonly understood to refer to the practice of Roman soldiers impressing civilians to carry their pack for a mile (it turns out this was relatively easy to measure, as Roman roads all had milestones). Jesus said if a Roman solider forced you to carry his pack for a mile, then rather than moaning about the injustice of it all – carry it an extra one! He challenges our natural response of grudging toleration. He moves us further on from simply choosing not to complain, into fully embracing the situation with generous acceptance.

If we demand or expect that people, places or events will make us happy, then we're miserable when they don't live up to our expectations. If we embrace what IS right now, without condition, and not only accept it, but "go the extra mile" we can welcome God's presence into what we are doing.

ACCEPTANCE ≠ PASSIVITY

Following the thought process on acceptance thus far, it is tempting to think of it as passivity or fatalism. We simply put up with what comes our way, and we do not fight against injustice. Nothing could be further from the truth. To illustrate this, let's look at the example of Nehemiah in the Old Testament

In the month of Kislev in the twentieth year, while I was in the citadel of Susa, Hanani, one of my brothers, came from Judah with some other men, and I questioned them about the Jewish remnant that had survived the exile, and also about Jerusalem. They said to me, "Those who survived the exile and are back in the province are in great

---

[8] Matthew 5:41

trouble and disgrace. The wall of Jerusalem is broken down, and its gates have been burned with fire." When I heard these things, I sat down and wept. For some days I mourned and fasted and prayed before the God of heaven.
[9]

Nehemiah received bad news: his people, which he knew to be God's people, were in trouble, living in a ruined city with few resources and little protection. Rather than sighing, thinking what a great pity it was and "what will be, will be", he did something about it. He started as we see here with fasting and praying for some days, seeking God on what was next, then reading on through the book we find he continued to pray, he planned, and he took committed action until he saw the change he believed God had called him to make. Perhaps he was inspired by the words of Psalm 112:

Surely the righteous will never be shaken; they will be remembered forever.

They will have no fear of bad news; their hearts are steadfast, trusting in the Lord.

Their hearts are secure, they will have no fear; in the end they will look in triumph on their foes. [10]

Stepping back for a moment. Let us suppose you find yourself in a situation you'd prefer not to be in. First question: is there an immediate opportunity to change the situation or leave the situation? If there is, presumably you would do it, and that is the end of the story. Take a trivial example: perhaps you are sitting on an uncomfortable chair – you get up and move to a different one and think no more about it. But if there isn't any immediate action

---

[9] Nehemiah 1:1-4
[10] Psalm 112:6-8

you can take; you've recognised that the situation will continue as-is for the time being and you need to deal with it. This is the case in all the examples we looked at: Paul's, the slaves', the impressed bag carrier.

At this point, why not stop any internal resistance and welcome God into what is happening right now? Now knowing we would prefer things to be different, as an intentional process we may make a plan towards one of two outcomes:

- We could effect change in the situation.
- We could leave the situation

These outcomes might be easily achieved, they make take considerable time, or may not be possible at all. Regardless of that, we can continue our acceptance - embracing what IS right now, and we can pray – talk it over with God. We discuss this later in talking about lament. Many times, unconditional acceptance and prayer will transform a situation in ways we could never have achieved on our own. And always, we will be better able to work from a place of clarity and insight to determine what, if any, action to take. This is beautifully expressed in the words of the "serenity prayer", attributed to Reinhold Neibuhr:

> *Lord grant me the serenity to accept the things I cannot change, the courage to change what I can, and the wisdom to know the difference.*

STUDY AND DISCUSSION QUESTIONS

1. Have you found times when it is difficult to determine if you should quietly go the extra mile, or speak up for change instead?

2. How often do you catch yourself complaining? What helps you overcome this?

3. What situations do you find particularly challenging to nurture acceptance in? How could you change this?

4. How can we best help others develop an attitude of acceptance?

CHAPTER 3

Beat the roadblocks

It is often the case that mental roadblocks get in our way as we start to explore the practice of acceptance. Here we explore the most common ones where our own thinking can trip us up.

OUR OWN WORST CRITIC

Transforming to an attitude of non-resistance brings more with it as well. A core part of acceptance is non-judgement. Fully accepting a situation means not judging the behaviour or motivations of others. If we find the present moment unacceptable, that is simply a label we are giving it, it is us sitting in judgement.

The same is true of judging ourselves as well as others. Often we are our own harshest critics, even let's say, when we are practising the presence of God, how easy is it to say: "I'm no good at this, I just keep failing", or "I let God down again by being judgemental".

One step towards this is accepting yourself the way you are at the moment – a work in progress. Christians believe that through the sacrifice of Jesus on the cross, God has already accepted and forgiven his followers, why not go with that? If you are carrying a heavy burden of guilt for example, and you can't seem to put it down – practice being accepting towards it. You've probably already tried reasoning with it: possibly you've had a conversation with yourself that went something like: "It says in the Bible my sins are forgiven so I don't need to hold onto this...". It is possible that the conversation was effective, but it is likely that it was not; winning a mental argument against your feelings can be quite challenging. Acceptance is different: we don't complain about our weakness or inability to change, we stop the fight, and choose to look at ourselves with love and compassion.

As is so often the case, we need to clarify what non-judgement is not. It does not mean you suspend critical thought or *check your brains at the door* [11] as one Christian author so aptly put it. When out and about, Jesus encouraged his disciples to be *"shrewd as snakes and as innocent as doves"* [12]. We are to be aware that others' agendas may not have our best interests at heart. They may lie and deceive at our expense and we need to be aware of the risks, but we retain an innocence where we do not become harsh or critical ourselves. We can still offer love and support to someone whilst being wary of their motives and actions.

Being judgemental of others is not our role. This does not mean that we don't recognise wrongdoing, acknowledge it as such, and if necessary, act to protect ourselves or others.

---

[11] Don't Check Your Brains At The Door by Josh McDowell, Bob Hostetler (Nelson 1992)
[12] Matthew 10:16

It is the difference between trying to fight the darkness in the dark or bringing in the light. It is avoiding reactivity and blame, and instead acting in love.

RELINQUISHMENT

Relinquishment. Hopefully, this is a word that sticks in your mind and is not simply bypassed and ignored. Relinquishment is a distinct part of the picture of acceptance, and it is about control.

I recently learned something about myself: it turns out I always like to know where I'm going. One day on summer vacation, my wife and I headed out for a walk. We were hiking through the forest, had nowhere particular we needed to be, no must-see sights on the doorstep – just a walk through the forest. She was happily walking, while I was looking at the map working out where we should end up. On being asked why I was looking at the map – I had no good answer. We were enjoying walking, why spoil it by worrying about the destination?

There are most certainly times when we want control of a situation – like crossing the road with our children, or operating dangerous machinery. But there are times when our need for knowing and control does not leave room for the presence of God.

Our Celtic Christian forbears had a name for a special type of pilgrimage, they called it *peregrinatio*. A call to journey with Christ, trusting him for the destination. There will be times when we are rightly pushing towards specific goals, but let us be open to the times when God calls us to journey with him without concern for anything but the next step.

An occasion I did successfully relinquish my need for control was my first time as a passenger on a friend's motorcycle. After our trip, he commented what an easy passenger I had been. Most people their first time on the back are very stiff and try to stay upright rather than relax and lean into the corners – trusting the rider and trusting the bike. Let us not miss opportunities to lean into the corners with God, trusting him for the outcome. This requires being comfortable with a mindset of not knowing, of accepting ambiguity. Not knowing the destination, not having all the answers to hand, but trusting the one who does. Saying "I don't know" can be difficult, especially if you are in a leadership role.

Scripture strongly encourages us to humility – being willing to admit we don't know everything and aren't in control. In several places the Bible says:

"God opposes the proud but shows favour to the humble." [13]

And we learn that:

...with humility comes wisdom. [14]

When we think of ourselves as "the expert", our minds are made up, it narrows our vision and reduces our capacity to act. Entering a situation with openness, with fresh eyes, brings new possibilities. We don't throw our knowledge away, it is waiting in the background for when we need it, but it is our servant not our master.

Having a "don't know" attitude and a willingness to cede control will make us wiser, as well as more open to God's presence.

---

[13] James 4:6b and 1 Peter 5:5 and Proverbs 3:34
[14] Proverbs 11:2b

THE QUESTION OF "WHY"

A common roadblock to acceptance is the question "why". This deserves our careful attention as it is more than capable of robbing us of our peace and our relationship with God.

When something difficult happens, we might start to think "if only", or perhaps start to ruminate on the question: "is this the will of God?", "surely God wouldn't want this?", "why hasn't anything changed yet?".

On that note, let us pause to talk about the will of God for a moment. Determining if something is the "will of God" is at least two quite distinct questions. You may ask if **actions you are considering** taking would be the will of God – something God would want you to do; or you may ask if what is **currently happening to you** is the will of God – something God chose to happen.

In terms of the first question – actions you control: your conduct, character, or life-choices, asking if something is the will of God is an excellent question; but looking at events in our lives, good and bad, and asking the same question is fraught with difficulty. Did God want something bad to happen to me? Was this because I did not obey him, or did not have enough faith, or made a poor choice – or is this simply what he selected for me? Despite what some teach, these are simply not helpful questions. On one level we all know choices have consequences – I do not pay the bills for example, and eventually people come knocking at the door; I cut corners at my job, and eventually I get fired. But we also see that life is unfair: the opportunities open to me are vastly different to those open to someone with similar abilities born in a third world country, or even a poor family in this country. The teacher in Ecclesiastes puts this rather brutally:

> *I have seen something else under the sun: The race is not to the swift or the battle to the strong, nor does food come to the wise or wealth to the brilliant or favour to the learned; but time and chance happen to them all.* [15]

Life has ups and downs, the teacher of Ecclesiastes says, which may be completely unrelated to the motivations and abilities of the one undergoing them. Looking at the letter of 1 Peter we find it suggests that punishment by the state could have directly opposite causes – either following the will of God or doing wrong[16]. In the world, the same activities can bring us persecution – or promotion!

If we can straightforwardly determine some cause and effect in a situation, well and good, we can learn from it and choose to act differently next time, but often we cannot easily do that. In those cases, would knowing the answer to the question "why" genuinely help us? We might think so, but if we are prepared to trust God, it turns out that it usually doesn't.

The "why" question does deserve some further attention, however. It is a struggle for me personally, because as my wife will clearly attest, "why" is probably my favourite word in the English language, and I've made a sport out of challenging any rule or policy I don't like, with the question "why". It is a natural human tendency to explore why things are the way they are, but when seeking the presence of God, it does not draw us closer. One of the best illustrations of this comes from one of the oldest books in the Bible – Job.

---

[15] Ecclesiastes 9:11
[16] 1 Peter 2:20

LESSONS FROM JOB

The opening section describes a series of calamities that befall Job: He loses his wealth, his family gets killed and then he loses his health also.

This is followed by about forty chapters of human reasoning on why Job's situation was the way it was. Four different humans spoke into this, in addition to Job. They represented age and experience, as well as youth and passion. They explored every avenue and yet did not find an answer to explain Job's suffering. Then to add to the frustration of someone like me who wants the "why", towards the end of the book God personally joined the conversation and did not offer an answer to the "why" question either. What God did do was ask some questions of his own, seventy-seven to be precise. These questions consistently point to the wonder of God and his creation.

Considering those forty chapters, this is a lot of Bible-space not to answer the question to which we might have been hoping for an answer. This sends a strong message: we will usually be wasting our time looking for an answer as to why we find ourselves in difficult situations. We are asking something beyond human reasoning.

Like most good stories, Job's does have a happy ending. It was not a rational explanation for what had happened to him, Job's resolution was in a bigger glimpse of God – and, as it happened, in the restitution of his life circumstances. Job said:

"My ear heard about you. Now my eyes see you." [17]

Job had heard about God, most likely the oral tradition in his family about what God was like. But Job has now added another

---

[17] Job 42:5

sense dimension: he has moved from hearing *about* God, to seeing him. His one-dimensional view of God has been upgraded. From knowing *about* God, to knowing God. He moved from a theoretical understanding of God's character to an experiential knowing of his presence. The same as one may know about a particular celebrity, their achievements, or their life story, which is very different from meeting them face to face and getting to know them as a person.

In my younger days, I tried to use theology to answer endless "why" questions. Whatever answers I got at best left me with a one-dimensional view of God for which I was poorer. Answering "why" may help us know about God, but it will not help us know him personally. This can be a difficult message to onboard, but it is core to Paul's "secret" of contentment. It turns out that "why" is often not a helpful question when we see that Job's peace came NOT from understanding, but beyond understanding, by a greater personal revelation of God to him.

WHEN "WHY" IS A GOOD QUESTION

We have talked about "why" not being a good question, so what about the times when it is? Perhaps a helpful lens to view this through is to recognise that asking "why" is typically our aid to solving problems – particularly problems we have some control over. Suppose you undertook a piece of work that turned out badly; or suppose you had a conversation with a friend and they went away upset; or suppose you are trying to learn a better way of doing a difficult task – in all these cases, understanding the "why" behind the way things happened can be very helpful. You can examine the underlying mechanisms of cause and effect, you can recognise wrong assumptions you made, or preconditions that affected the outcome. All of these can help you make better choices in similar situations in the future. This stands in contrast to seeking the presence of God. Asking "why" can deflect us from relationship with him because God is not a problem to be solved.

A QUICK RECAP

Unconditional acceptance is a choice of the will, a mental and spiritual discipline. Once understood, it is a straightforward choice – a day by day, hour by hour, minute by minute decision. It does not require special intelligence or ability. It is within the grasp of all of us.

The challenge is to start from a place of acceptance whatever the situation and welcome God into the here and now in your life. Whatever the situation includes *everything*: **people** – the good and the bad ones; **circumstances** – situations you enjoy and those you don't; and **yourself** – your identity, your thoughts and your feelings.

Watch out for inner resistance – like complaining, or judgement, or desire for control, and seek to gently set them down. As humans we like to fix things, and get stuff done, and that's right and good – but let's start by seeking to welcome God into all our different life situations without resisting, complaining and judging, but by accepting, then we will be free indeed.

STUDY AND DISCUSSION QUESTIONS

1. Are there any times when you have found the question "why" useful when it comes to facing difficult circumstances? What made it useful?

2. Recognising that life is never completely fair, how does that affect your approach to social justice issues?

3. In what circumstances do you find it difficult to not be in control? Does it matter?

4. Do you find it difficult to set aside being critical of yourself or others? How could it be easier?

5. How can we best balance loving acceptance of others whilst recognising their motives may not be pure?

CHAPTER 4

Hey... over here!

DISTRACTIONS ABOUND

B efore I sat down to work this morning, I ended up watching a time-lapse video showing how to make an epoxy coffee table. I do not need a new coffee table; I had no intention of making this coffee table; I am not particularly interested in coffee tables; and it turned out to be an ugly coffee table in the end anyway. Why did I watch it? I don't know, but I did, and for those few minutes I gave away my attention to something that added nothing to my life or anyone else's. I didn't even feel more relaxed or achieved afterward. My mental puppy had headed off and was running in circles around the yard.

We all have a precious gift that is ours to give every moment of the day – our attention. This is the primary currency of the marketing and social media worlds and it is something we so easily give away without a second thought. We've all experienced social interactions where we can tell that we do not have the other person's attention. This can come across anywhere from mildly unhelpful to downright rude. But even when we do give our attention, it is many times only at a surface level, and is not sustained, intentional mental direction.

For most of us, we are so accustomed to living a distracted life we do not even notice that we are distracted. Jesus said of some of his listeners that *Though seeing, they do not see; though hearing, they do not hear or understand.* [18] We can see and hear, but the true depth and meaning can completely pass us by.

INTRODUCING THE WATCHER

We'll explore now how God encourages us to take back control of our attention and choose where and how we direct it. The book of Proverbs speaks directly to this issue:

> *Watch over your heart with all diligence, for from it flow the springs of life.* [19]

Scripture uses the word heart to refer to a person's innermost thoughts and feelings. There is a key phrase here which is "watch over". Many translations have "guard", and a guard, will, of course watch over the thing guarded. We are encouraged then to watch over our heart, the deepest part of our life, our innermost thoughts and feelings. Many streams of spirituality as well as psychotherapy would encourage the same: we recognise that there is a part of ourselves that can step back and watch our thoughts, feelings and circumstances. Sometimes this is called the "observing self" or the "watcher". It is a definite, distinct capability that we have – attested to by ancient scripture and modern science. This terminology is somewhat illustrative and metaphorical as the watcher is not a separate "self" but rather the

---

[18] Matthew 13:13
[19] Proverbs 4:23 (NASB)

truth that there is part of you able to step back and watch what you are thinking. Some may think of this as "soul", but we will not get distracted here by trying to explain it.

For some, there is a natural fear of looking inwards. The thought of self-examination does not sound appealing. Yet as we explore this more deeply, we will discover that the issue is not in itself that of looking inwards, but how we respond to what we find. This could be with compassion on one hand or with judgement on the other, but a good starting place is a simple acknowledgement of our thoughts and feelings – deliberately avoiding any kind of analysis. Some 2500 years after these words in Proverbs were penned, modern psychotherapy has realised the benefits of intentional attention and called it mindfulness. This can be attention on our own thoughts and feelings, attention on our body or attention on what is happening around us. An attention that is a simple non-judgemental awareness without analysis or commentary.

Mindfulness does not specify a particular thing to attend to, it is simply the act of intentionally directing your attention. It can be useful to think of attention like a spotlight: you can direct it all around your body to different places; or you can direct it around your surroundings, even picking one of your senses like hearing, smell or touch and noticing what's there; or as in the Proverbs verse we just reviewed, you can direct it at your mind – and notice the flow of thoughts and feelings that is going on.

DON'T SLEEPWALK

Scripture not only encourages us to watch over our own heart, but also to watch out for what the Lord may want of us. There is a beautiful illustration in the Psalms that is often missed as we haven't understood the customs and practices of the time.

As the eyes of slaves look to the hand of their master, as
the eyes of a female slave look to the hand of her mistress,
so our eyes look to the LORD our God... [20]

If you were the servant on duty, you would often stand quietly in the room, ready to respond to a simple hand-signal from the master that something needed doing. Although this may be not something we would expect or condone today, it is a perfect illustration of what quiet, sustained attention looks like.

The theme occurs in other Psalms also: *My eyes are always on the LORD...*[21] and *my eyes are fixed on You, O GOD* [22] . We see a pattern in the scripture of sustained attention on God. Many have missed the subtlety, but the New Testament speaks to this process extensively. Here are some examples:

When Jesus is praying in the garden of Gethsemane before he is arrested, he invites his closest disciples to "*Stay here and keep watch with me.*" [23]. Jesus is seeking support while he prays, and the disciples are invited to "keep watch", not to offer busy wordy prayers, but give quiet sustained attention.

Paul's letter to the Colossians has this instruction: *Devote yourselves to prayer, being watchful and thankful* [24]. Alongside a continued devotion to prayer, Paul says to do this in a way that keeps your attention focused.

We see a similar theme in other of Paul's letters. 1 Thessalonians says: *so then let us not sleep as others do, but let us be alert and sober* [25]. Here the state of attentive watchfulness is contrasted with "sleeping". It is clear in the context that this is not

---

[20] Psalm 123:2
[21] Psalm 25:15
[22] Psalm 141:8
[23] Matthew 26:38
[24] Colossians 4:2
[25] 1 Thessalonians 5:6

physically sleeping, but rather figuratively sleepwalking through life: being led around by your thoughts and feelings without any real awareness that it is happening. For many of us, it is commonplace to sleepwalk through our days much of the time without sustained awareness of what's going on in our hearts.

This quiet, sustained attention is also called "waiting on the Lord" – the phrase comes up some thirty times in the Bible, and speaks to us being ready for him and available to him; this is the true source of our strength as the prophet Isaiah attests:

> *Yet those who wait for the Lord will gain new strength; They will mount up with wings like eagles, They will run and not get tired, They will walk and not become weary.* [26]

---

[26] Isaiah 40:31 NASB

STUDY AND DISCUSSION QUESTIONS

1. Does the idea of the "watcher" or "observing self" sit easily with you? What are your experiences of playing the role of watcher?

2. What are your most challenging distractions: Internal - like difficult thoughts? Or External – like social media?

3. Is it practical and/or helpful to stay focused and aware all the time?

4. Can distractions be positive and relaxing? What makes them so?

5. If you're trying to avoid being distracted, what helps you do that?

CHAPTER 5

How to make it count

Shortly we will dive into the first set of practical exercises, but before doing so, I would like to talk briefly about how to approach them, how to make them work for you. The concepts in this book are for the most part straightforward to grasp, but mastering their practice can be a lifetime endeavour, so regularly returning to practice and being flexible in our approach to what works for each of us is essential. Some concepts and practices may be familiar to you, some may feel entirely foreign, but I would encourage you to make time to try each of them out, determine which will serve you best in your spiritual journey then build them into your life.

Each exercise is described prescriptively so it is easy to follow and get started, but in no case should the exercise method be seen as a "formula" which is the only way to get results. The descriptions are examples to get you started.

It is often the case that starting out can seem a little daunting. It can be helpful to work with a buddy or a group for mutual support. It is very unlikely but also possible that some of this work might raise awareness of past trauma. If you find yourself being triggered by any of the exercises, please stop immediately and seek professional support.

Some writers have separated spiritual practices between personal and corporate – I have not done that here. Almost all the practical exercises suggested can be done alone or with others but will usually benefit from community interaction. It will be especially valuable if you are able to form a small support group to grow in these practices. Early Christians lived in cultures with strong communities, in contrast to our modern more individualistic culture. This means that we tend to find our bias is towards personal, rather than corporate spiritual growth and we will benefit from being intentional in seeking a balance between the two.

All the practices described need a starting point. These starting points come in two types:

- Scheduled or planned

- Situational or prompted

Scheduled time is just that: planning in time to complete the work, anything from a few minutes upward. For anyone serious about growing spiritually, scheduled time is essential. We plan in time to eat, work and meet with friends, so why not plan in time for spiritual things? Jesus and his followers made it a habit to set aside time, seeking quiet, uninterrupted space to meet with God. The exact times and places are irrelevant – what will work for you?

The second type of starting point is a situational prompt. Many of the practices in this book come to life when applied in the busyness of everyday life, but when we're wrapped up in life situations the tendency is to forget, and to look back afterwards and think: "If only I'd remembered to...". A way to overcome this is to have an event or common situation that will remind you of the practice – a prompt or trigger. This can be anything from walking through a door to waiting in traffic. It takes time and effort for us to embed prompts like this in our lives. It's helpful not to focus on more than one or two at any given time and use things like your scheduled time to remind yourself of the triggers you want to pick up on. Try visual cues like sticky notes in the car.

Do also bear in mind that this is not schoolwork – with most of the exercises there is no right or wrong. Making room for God's presence in our lives is a lifetime journey and these exercises are designed to be helpful steps on your path.

Acceptance and Attention

Having introduced the core themes, here is some practical groundwork. Many of the later exercises depend on these, so please do start here. Some of the exercises in the book may not seem particularly "spiritual" to you but don't be fooled, whenever we cultivate unconditional loving acceptance and quiet, sustained attention there is inevitably a spiritual dimension and we will be growing our ability to make room for God's presence.

Exercise I.   CHECK ON THE PUPPY

For this exercise, take time to stop and mentally ask yourself: "what am I thinking right now?" and then watch the result. Regularly take a few minutes for this. Be at least as interested in what's going on inside your head, as what's going on outside. Step back and deliberately notice the thoughts that drift through your head. This is a version of what would commonly be called a mindfulness practice in today's language.

You may find your mind is actually quiet for a while which can be a great blessing; or it may head straight off running in circles like a puppy. Whatever happens, focus on being the observer and avoid getting caught up in a train of thought. Aim to be a curious scientist watching an experiment and simply note what's going on. Your thoughts and feelings may be ones you'd wish to have or you may not like them – don't be judgemental, just observe. By watching the mechanics of the mind you can step out of unhelpful thought patterns.

If you find time has passed and you suddenly realise you were completely caught up (hint: this happens a lot) then don't criticise yourself, simply return to the observation post and get back to watching.

This is a powerful practice which exercises both attention and acceptance and will naturally develop separation between you and your thoughts and feelings.

Exercise II.   LEAN IN

If you notice a difficult thought or feeling (whether you were looking for it or not) then don't push it away. This might be anxiety, or resentment, or annoyance – whatever it is doesn't matter. Acknowledge it and watch it.

As you're watching it, go beyond a disinterested watching to active compassion: imagine this difficult thought or feeling is a crying baby and offer it love and comfort.

If what is going on in your mind translates into a feeling in your physical body – like a tenseness in your gut for example, then imagine surrounding that part of your body with love, warmth and light. Simply allow it to be and be compassionate towards it.

Suppressing difficult thoughts and feelings usually means they come back bigger and nastier later. Jesus tells us to have compassion and that there is no condemnation – let's start that command with ourselves; over time the baby will stop crying and the following quietness makes it easier for us to hear God.

Exercise III.   CHECK YOUR ACCEPTANCE LEVEL

A challenge for each of us can be to know if we have fully accepted our present situation. Although you would not have chosen many situations you find yourself in, see if you can accept the current situation it <u>as if you had chosen it.</u>

Did you catch yourself complaining – either vocally or in your head? Or is there an unwillingness to be in your present situation or a resentment of people around you? Would you rather be somewhere else? Maybe the situation isn't great, someone around you is annoying, or you've been badly treated. It makes no difference how "justified" you feel, the fact is you are mentally fighting against life.

So, if it makes sense to speak up, to change the situation or move away – do it NOW; if that's not immediately possible, then set down your complaint. It is a heavy bag you don't need and it puts barriers between you and God's presence. Put down the bag. Embrace the situation fully and look to go the extra mile if you can.

If the heavy bag seems welded to your arm and you're struggling to put it down, then go to the previous exercise and *Lean In* to it. Also check out the later exercise on *Lamenting Well*.

PART 2

PLOTTING PATHWAYS

*Where we explore the five pathways of stillness,
present moment, place, praise, and prayer; and
discover how they can be shaped to work for you.*

CHAPTER 6

Slowing it down

Psalm 46 is a well-known but little practised verse, an invitation to slow down and explore the pathway of stillness:

"Be still, and know that I am God"... [27]

Start by being still, we are told, then move onto knowing God. Without making room through stillness, the presence of God can easily be crowded out in our heads, and therefore our lives. This Psalm invites us to get to know God better personally through the practice of stillness.

There are many ways to put this stillness into practice and we will explore three main ones: simple stillness, meditating on God's Word, and meditating on God's works. Some will feel naturally more comfortable to you than others, but all are worth testing out.

Scripture refers often to the idea of meditation. Meditation is a tool we can use to encourage stillness: to quieten our noisy brains and focus our attention on the Lord. When some hear the

---

27 Psalm 46:10

word "meditation", the immediate thoughts that come to mind involve chanting and sitting cross-legged on the floor, and they do not think of it as a Christian practice. Nothing could be further from the truth – the idea of meditation occurs dozens of times in the Bible starting from Genesis; the book of Psalms opens with a meditation promise, saying that things will go well for the one who meditates "day and night" on the law of the Lord.

Meditation, very simply, is us taking control of our attention and directing it consistently in a planned direction. But what should we meditate on and how should we start? We will explore three primary paths.

SIMPLE STILLNESS

"Not to be able to stop thinking is a dreadful affliction"

Eckhard Tole

We often think of Christian devotions as busy-ness – reading the Bible, thinking through what to pray about, praying fervently. We also need to "be still" to create the space to know God. God is our heavenly Father – if we make space, why would he not meet with us?

Talking about taking time with God, David says in the Psalms:

"I have calmed and quieted my soul like a weaned child with its mother..." [28]

The Bible also describes this process as "waiting on God":

For God alone my soul waits in silence; [29]

---

[28] Psalm 131:2
[29] Psalm 62:1

And:

The Lord is good to those who wait for him, to the soul who seeks him. It is good that one should wait on the Lord quietly [30]

These are an invitation into a simple stillness and quiet with God. Making space for him without questions, demands or a running commentary. Many Christians' idea of a prayer meeting is talking and talking to God, and when you are not talking, you are thinking about the next thing you're going to talk about. Jesus challenges those who think God hears them better for their many words to think again[31]. There is most definitely space for verbal prayer in Christian practice, but when it becomes the only approach to God, we can drown out his presence with our noise.

Some churches' worship times do include times of silence, but silence on the outside does not imply silence on the inside. That is a choice we need to make, and it will take time to nurture. Growing up attending a Quaker school, a friend of mine discovered this by having to regularly sit in silence for fifteen minutes as part of corporate worship. As an eleven-year-old, he found this boring and frustrating, but over several years, he noticed a shift to where he welcomed and appreciated the space. Without any formal instruction he learned to reflect the outer stillness into inner stillness.

With our typical busy brains, we can find this most simple of invitations the most difficult. A common practice to developing this stillness is to choose an undisturbed place to sit, and just allow ourselves to be quiet. If thoughts come to our mind, we let them pass rather than clinging on to them and trying to solve the

---

[30] Lamentations 3:25–26
[31] Matthew 6:7

next problem. It can be helpful to focus on your breathing – slowly breathing in and out and directing your attention solely to that. Breath is a powerful choice of focus. It was God's giving of life in Genesis:

> *Then the Lord God formed a man from the dust of the ground and breathed into his nostrils the breath of life, and the man became a living being.*[32]

It was Jesus' invitation to receive the Holy Spirit:

> *And with that he breathed on them and said, "Receive the Holy Spirit.*[33]

In both Greek and Hebrew, the primary original languages of the Bible, the same word is used for "breath" and "spirit" – they both bring life and are both identified with the presence of God, so a focus on breath naturally focuses on God as the life-giver, and the Spirit as a presence within us.

If you find it helpful, you can consider breathing in as receiving a refreshing of God's Holy Spirit, and breathing out as a release of all you don't need: fears, worries, hurt and guilt. But don't over-think it, my usual practice is to keep a simple attention on the breath.

MEDITATION ON GOD'S WORD

The scriptures are full of invitations for us to meditate on God's Word, the Bible. As mentioned before, the book of Psalms opens with an encouragement to meditation and a promise that things will go well when that becomes your practice.

---

[32] Genesis 2:7
[33] John 20:22

Blessed is the man who walks not in the counsel of the wicked, nor stands in the way of sinners, nor sits in the seat of scoffers; but his delight is in the law of the Lord, and on his law he meditates day and night. He is like a tree planted by streams of water that yields its fruit in its season, and its leaf does not wither. In all that he does, he prospers. [34]

It is helpful to see here that meditation is part of a lifestyle of good character, not a standalone activity, and the "blessed man" meditates "day and night" – it's an ongoing pattern, not limited to attendance at a quiet retreat centre.

This promise is repeated from one given to Joshua where again, there's a clear link to lifestyle: putting into practice what you meditate about.

This Book of the Law shall not depart from your mouth, but you shall meditate on it day and night, so that you may be careful to do according to all that is written in it. For then you will make your way prosperous, and then you will have good success. [35]

Meditation on scripture is quite different to studying scripture. Studying involves analysis and research. With meditation we are allowing the scripture to work on us, rather than us working on the scripture. Treating it as the living Word of Christ - a gift to be received rather than a problem to be solved. The historic theologian Thomas Cranmer said of scripture meditation:

"Let us ruminate, and, as it were, chew the cud, that we may have the sweet juice, spiritual effect, marrow, honey, kernel, taste, comfort and consolation of them."

---

[34] Psalm 1:1-3
[35] Joshua 1:8

There are endless combinations of ways to meditate on God's Word – the ancient practice of *Lectio Divina* is a well-established framework. Pioneered by early Christian scholars from the 3rd century, including Origen, Ambrose and Augustine, it became rooted in monastic tradition by Benedict in the 6th century and was seen as a key to nourishing Christian spirituality.

The essential core to *Lectio* is the attitude and approach to scripture. At its heart, the design is firstly to encourage connection with God through scripture, and secondly for any learning to become embedded in lifestyle. Exactly the pattern indicated in the Bible passages above.

Before starting, a passage of the Bible needs to be selected. This is usually fairly short but could be anything from a single verse to a full narrative section. Historically it was done in a community setting and could last anything from twenty minutes to several hours. The details of each step varied a little from community to community but traditional *Lectio* has four steps that have been likened to enjoying a meal – taking a bite, chewing it, savouring its essence, and digesting it.

The practical section explains the how-to in detail along with another common approach, that of narrative engagement.

MEDITATION ON GOD'S WORKS

Perhaps less often seen as a spiritual practice but clearly found in scripture is meditation on the works of God. Here's a few examples from Psalms:

> *Great are the works of the Lord; they are pondered by all who delight in them.* [36]

---

[36] Psalm 111:2

I will ponder all your work, and meditate on your mighty deeds. [37]

I remember the days of old; I meditate on all that you have done; I ponder the work of your hands. [38]

Cause me to understand the way of your precepts, that I may meditate on your wonderful deeds. [39]

Perhaps this is a less common practice among Christians because there is a worry about "worshipping the creation rather than the creator" [40] and our faith somehow becoming a nature religion. Surely this is a case of throwing out the baby with the bathwater, the examples we have seen speak clearly.

But why would we meditate on God's works? As Psalm 19 states: *The heavens declare the glory of God; the skies proclaim the work of his hands.*[41] Just as we saw with Job, the believer is directed to God's works to appreciate his greatness and glory.

I had a friend professing no faith, who was completing a climbing challenge by cresting Scafell Pike in the English Lake District as darkness fell. Reaching the top, he saw the full moon rising on a clear sky, and said in that moment he thought how could there not be a God? I have felt the same hiking in the mountains of Oregon and stepping from the forest into a clearing and seeing the peak of Mount Hood reflected in the lake in front of me. Even in the everyday, from the invisible beauty of the human genome to the engineering marvel of a spider turning dead flies into resilient complex structures. The wonder of creation is everywhere we look.

---

[37] Psalm 77:12
[38] Psalm 143:5
[39] Psalm 119:27
[40] Romans 1:25 paraphrase
[41] Psalm 19.1

How and when?

As we think about stillness and meditation, a natural picture is that of a quiet space where we carry out this practice. Some specific practices like Lectio Divina will require that, and we see, for example in the life of Jesus how he would carve out quiet space to connect with his heavenly Father. But this is not the whole story. Many of the references to meditating on God's Word talk about "day and night" – a continual practice as part of day to day living. Perhaps most telling is Psalm 46 where we started with the famous phrase "be still". Reviewing the whole Psalm makes it abundantly clear that stillness is not reserved for quiet places.

The Psalm starts with this encouragement:

God is our refuge and strength, an ever-present help in trouble. Therefore we will not fear, though the earth give way and the mountains fall into the heart of the sea, though its waters roar and foam and the mountains quake with their surging. [42]

It also tells us:

Nations are in uproar, kingdoms fall; he lifts his voice, the earth melts. [43]

On the outside there are wars, earthquakes and desolation – yet God invites us to enter stillness with him. Yes, we may choose to practice stillness on a quiet, meditative retreat, but where it really counts is when we can maintain the same stillness when the world is collapsing around us.

Stillness is setting aside our own agenda, the busyness and distractions of the day, the past, the future and allowing space for

---

[42] Psalm 46:1-2
[43] Psalm 46:5

God right now. This inside stillness is in no way dependent on the circumstances around us. This stillness is not due to incredible mental feats of discipline on our part – but as we choose stillness and make room for his presence, He brings peace and rest.

PEACE AND REST

The Bible talks about both peace and rest and it is helpful to consider these in light of stillness.

Peace is used in at least two ways in the Bible. Firstly, it describes relationship: Romans 5 says *Therefore, since we have been justified through faith, we have peace with God through our Lord Jesus Christ.* Because of the work of Christ, there is no war between us and God – we are at peace.

Then secondly, it describes an inner calm available to us **because** of the relationship we have with God, the *peace of God, which surpasses all understanding*, as Paul's Philippian letter describes it. As we talked about earlier, this peace of God does not come from a better understanding of our situation, answering the "why" question; it is a peace that is beyond understanding as a direct result of our relationship with him. As we find pathways into his presence, we will see our relationship of peace come more and more to the fore in our lives. As we break the relationship with him, peace recedes far from us, as the prophet Isaiah said: *the wicked are like the tossing sea, which cannot rest.* [44]

Rest is closely related. In the Bible, "rest" can be used to mean simple refreshing and relaxation, but it often has a subtler meaning. The first usage in the Bible is God "resting" when finishing creation.[45] He did not rest because He was tired, but this

---

[44] Isaiah 57:20
[45] Genesis 2:2

rest was a state of completeness, where everything is as it should be.

True rest comes from being in God's presence. He said as much to Moses:

My Presence will go with you, and I will give you rest. [46]

This is the same rest that Jesus offered to the weary and burdened – a place of refreshing where everything is as it should be. The Hebrews letter encourages us to find this place of rest:

Let us, therefore, make every effort to enter that rest, [47]

How will we make every effort? By finding pathways into his presence.

---

[46] Exodus 33:14
[47] Hebrews 4:11a

STUDY AND DISCUSSION QUESTIONS

1. How easy do you find it to maintain inner stillness when you are quiet and alone – and what helps you the most?

2. How easy do you find it to maintain the same stillness when the world is collapsing around you – and what helps you the most?

3. Have you tried meditation – what were your experiences?

4. Which forms of meditation do you relate most easily to and why? (Simple stillness, God's word, God's works, or something else)

5. What can you do to better recognise God works (as creator and sustainer) in everyday life?

PRACTICAL PAUSE
Stillness

Exercise IV. SIMPLE STILLNESS

P lease invest time in this exercise, it lays the groundwork for many exercises in the book, and techniques I describe here I have not repeated later.

For this exercise it is valuable to find a quiet space and set aside a fixed amount of time. Start with five minutes or so and work up from there. It's best to take a comfortable but alert pose: usually seated and relaxed but with a straight back and feet flat on the floor. It's also handy to have a pen and paper nearby.

It may be helpful to start with a short prayer, I have found this one written by Christine Sine to be helpful:

Lord help me to live simply
To give my life and all I am into your hands
Help me to unclutter my closet
For I have too much stuff that takes me away from your presence

Help me to unclutter my calendar
For I am often too busy to focus my attention on you
Help me to unclutter my mind
For I have too many unguided thoughts
That distract me from your instructions [48]

Then close your eyes and take slow, deep breaths. If you are able to hold mental stillness without focusing on anything then do it, but most people find it easier to focus on their breath. There can be a particularly effective point of stillness putting your attention on the pause at the end of your out-breath. If you prefer not to focus on your breath, you can recite a very simple prayer, such as "Come, Lord Jesus".

You will find wayward thoughts popping up. This will happen a lot. The secret is not to get hooked by them into an extended mental narrative. I frequently end up trying to solve some workplace problem when I do this. When you notice a thought pop up, try not to hold onto it, but neither try to push it away. The very act of trying to un-think something simply brings our attention back to it. What if I say to you DON'T think about elephants. How does that play out?

Some people find helpful the idea of imagining the thought blowing away in the wind, or placing it on a leaf and letting it float downstream.

When you (inevitably) do get caught up in a train of thought and notice a couple of minutes later that you lost the plot, don't worry, just reset and focus back on your breathing.

I have found there are times when it can be helpful to break the exercise. Firstly, if a "to do" item pops up in your mind and you are worried you might forget about it, then pause and write it

---

[48] Christine Sine. godspace.wordpress.com

down. It is much easier to do that and forget about it, than have it keep popping up.

Secondly, some crazy, wonderful, inspirational idea might come up, possibly fully formed and apparently out of nowhere – you may want to make a note of it. If you have taken time to be still in God's presence, then could it be he might speak to you? It would be a shame to miss it because you were so busy trying to be still.

I often do this exercise while walking and make voice notes on my phone if the need arises.

This practice is a balance between flexibility and willingness to adapt on one hand and not allowing our puppy mind to run off and call the shots on the other hand.

This can be used at a regular scheduled time such as a short daily practice; it can also be extremely helpful during the busyness of the day, such as taking a one minute stillness pause before you start a new piece of work.

Exercise V. LECTIO DIVINA

This is a well-established method for meditating on God's Word and has four steps: *Lectio* ("read"), *Meditatio* ("meditate"), *Oratio* ("pray"), *Contemplatio* ("contemplate"). Different traditions have slightly different details in their practice, and it is wise to be open to what works for you, rather than slavishly following a process.

Firstly, is the need to pick a passage. It can be anything from a single verse to a longer narrative section. I would suggest not making it too long. If you follow any programme of Bible readings, this can be used as a prompt, or you may wish to focus on a particular topic.

Here are the four steps which you will aim to cover in around twenty minutes.

Lectio ("read")

Read really slowly through the passage several times. Get to know what's there. Don't try and analyse, just absorb. Don't force it, but listen carefully for any phrases that stand out to you.

Meditatio ("meditate")

Focus on any parts that have stood out to you and hold them in your mind, ponder them rather than analyse.

Oratio ("pray")

An opportunity to respond to God. Play back your impressions on the passage to God, talk it over with him. Some people choosing to journal at this point.

Contemplatio ("contemplate")

Complete the exercise by spending time quietly resting in God.

Although this can be done by yourself, it can be rewarding as part of a group exercise – I most often do this in small groups in the home. There is then opportunity to share with others what God has been saying to you, and if appropriate for your setting, taking the opportunity to hold each other accountable for actions you plan to take.

Exercise VI.   NARRATIVE ENGAGEMENT

This is another approach to Bible meditation that applies especially to narrative passages. It is wise to allow at least twenty minutes as with *lectio*, but you could spend considerably longer.

In this approach, you use your imagination as a tool to immerse yourself in the story. Your goal is to enter the story as an active participant rather than a passive observer. Having read through the passage slowly, close your eyes and picture the scene using as many senses as you can. See the landscape and the people, feel the heat of the day, the coarseness of your clothing, the hardness of the ground. Consider the sounds around you: people talking, animal noises. Try putting yourself in the shoes of different participants of the story as it proceeds – ask yourself what are you thinking and feeling?

Then move on to response – what has God shown you? You could imagine yourself sitting down with Jesus and talking it over with him. You may just be quietly content in his presence, or you may need to take action. It is usually helpful to have a journal available to note down any impressions you have.

Exercise VII. CREATION APPRECIATION

As scripture repeatedly encourages us, it is good to spend time meditating on God's works and his creation. There is really no limit on how to approach this. As an example, you can take time when out walking to simply absorb the wonder of God's creation. Take intentional attention and direct it to everything around – from the smallest flower to the largest mountain. Wherever you are, it is hard not to notice man-made things alongside natural beauty – don't let this bother you and remember that Christ is *sustaining all things by his powerful word.* [49]

As with scripture meditation, do not attempt to analyse, dissect or understand – simply observe and marvel at the wonder of our creator God.

---

[49] Hebrews 1:3

A natural tendency of the human brain is to start ignoring signals that come in regularly over time. When you sit in a chair, for example, you soon ignore the feeling of being seated. If you start wearing a watch, you soon forget you are wearing it. This process extends beyond our senses to all kinds of experiences which we are quick to normalise. This goes a long way to explaining much of humanities' dissatisfactions: yesterday's special treat, is today's expectation, becomes tomorrow's "not enough". Natural though this is, we can interrupt the process with intentional attention. We stop and deliberately choose to appreciate – perhaps imagining that we are experiencing it for the very first time. This can turn the most seemingly ordinary experiences into precious moments.

CHAPTER 7

The only time that matters

PRESENCE IMPLIES THE PRESENT

Sometimes it can be tempting to seek God in some future thing, or in the past – but his presence is here and now, "presence" implies this. If you are present – it means you are here – not elsewhere, and you're here now – not at some other time. So pause and think on this: the ONLY place you can connect with God is here, and now. In a very real sense, *now* is the only time that matters. On one level, this seems completely obvious, but perhaps it is so obvious that we miss it. We are seeking God in some special place or some special time, missing the reality that we cannot connect with God other than here and now. So why not here and why not now? The contemplative Christian author Richard Rohr expressed it like this:

> *"When you can be present, you will know the real Presence. I promise you this is true. And it is almost that simple."*

Imagine you strike up a casual conversation with a stranger: you chat for a short while, then having thoroughly discussed the weather in true British fashion, you carry on with your day and think no more about it. Would the conversation have been different if you had realised that the stranger was a celebrity in disguise, one of your heroes? A successful author / athlete / scientist / influencer? In the same vein, would our perspective on life be different if we recognised God at work in the most trivial and also the most traumatic of times?

If you have invested time in the "Check on the puppy" exercise you may well have been surprised at how much mental time is spent *outside* of the present moment: solving problems that haven't happened yet and probably never will, or re-hashing past situations that cannot be changed. Our brains love to solve problems: from crosswords to Minecraft™, but neither past nor future problems can be solved right now.

We imagine the past defines our identity and the future contains our hope, but both the future and the past can distract us from the reality of God's presence right here, right now. Let us look at each in turn:

THE PERILS OF THE PAST

> *"the person who puts his hand to the plough and looks back is not fit for the kingdom of God...."* [50]

Jesus said these words in a teaching session with his disciples. On the surface it seems quite a harsh statement on someone unsure of their life direction or maybe having a bit of a wobble. But what if it is a simple statement of fact with immediate

---

[50] Luke 9:62

application? If you are looking backward, you cannot engage with God. You cannot be in his presence if you are focusing on the past. This is true of positive as well as negative past experiences: the book of Ecclesiastes says: *don't long for the good old days – this is not wise.* [51]

Unless you are in the middle of a time-travel movie there is one sure thing about the past: it cannot be changed. A lot of unhelpful emotions have their home in the past – regret, resentment, guilt, unforgiveness. Things we are holding onto that have been done to us or we have done. These repeating narratives in our heads keep us from God's presence. Jesus speaks directly to this issue in the Sermon on the Mount:

> *So if you are offering your gift at the altar and there remember that your brother has something against you, leave your gift there before the altar. First go and be reconciled to your brother; then come and offer your gift.* [52]

We cannot worship meaningfully whilst holding on to our past unforgiveness.

So what do we do with a heavy bag that is weighing us down? The simple answer is put it down, stop carrying it around with you. How then, do we translate that to putting down our past burdens of guilt and unforgiveness? Is it that simple? Sometimes it can be, as our problem has been a lack of awareness of what's going on in our minds, and when we become aware of it, then we are able to set aside such negative thinking. At other times, it may be considerably more difficult as the stories of the wrong done to us, or we have done to others continues to circle around in our heads – much like the puppy running in circles in the garden.

---

[51] Ecclesiastes 7:10
[52] Matthew 5:23-24

Reasoning with these errant thoughts is much like trying to reason with the puppy: sometimes you don't want to let the story go, you deserve the right to hold onto it; or perhaps you try to argue with yourself that it's wrong and you are free in Christ but your mind doesn't agree. Either way, it is likely to leave you feeling exhausted and more guilty – meanwhile the puppy is still circling the garden.

There is a different way –
Unconditional Acceptance and Intentional Attention.

We become the watcher, we step back to the observing part of the mind and look at this story circling our mind, much as a curious scientist might. We don't judge or condemn this story – God has told us not to judge ourselves, we're compassionate towards it, as God loved us, even when we were a mess. We bring the light of God's presence, and the darkness will evaporate.

One compelling reason for many of us to cling to the past, is that we feel it determines who we are now – our identity. All of our successes, failures and experiences have made us the person we are, so why would we try and write them off?

The Bible speaks very clearly on this – our real identity is in Christ. To make the point, it uses the powerful illustration of dying and returning to life. Paul says we were "crucified with Christ" and now we are "a new creation". The things that defined who we were before don't matter: the bad and unhelpful things have been cleaned away by the power of Jesus and the good and the great things don't make us any more worthy to God – he loves us just the same. The past does not define our true identity – God does.

You may start to see that you have far less need for the past than you may think but it does have some uses. Here are two specific ones. Firstly, there may be opportunities to learn from the past. For example, you may reflect on how a difficult situation was managed – what worked, what didn't work, what could have been done differently. Secondly reflecting on what God has done – like Psalm 143 - *I remember the days of old, I think about all your deeds...* In both of these cases recalling the past is intentional and purposeful – not a constant mental replay of a well-worn narrative.

THE FICTION OF THE FUTURE

Do you rely on the future for your fulfillment? Returning to the Sermon on the Mount, Jesus speaks clearly about how we should view the future:

> *Therefore I tell you, do not worry about your life, what you will eat or drink; or about your body, what you will wear. Is not life more than food, and the body more than clothes? Look at the birds of the air; they do not sow or reap or store away in barns, and yet your heavenly Father feeds them. Are you not much more valuable than they? Can any one of you by worrying add a single hour to your life?*
>
> *And why do you worry about clothes? See how the flowers of the field grow. They do not labour or spin. Yet I tell you that not even Solomon in all his splendour was dressed like one of these. If that is how God clothes the grass of the field, which is here today and tomorrow is thrown into the fire, will he not much more clothe you—you of little faith? So do not worry, saying, 'What shall we eat?' or 'What shall we drink?' or 'What shall we wear?' For the pagans run after all these things, and your heavenly Father knows that you need them.*
>
> *But seek first his kingdom and his righteousness, and all these things will be given to you as well. Therefore do not*

worry about tomorrow, for tomorrow will worry about itself. Each day has enough trouble of its own. [53]

Jesus puts on display basic human needs, and asks pointed rhetorical questions: Will it improve your life to worry about where these are coming from? Will it make your life any longer? He uses the examples of other living things like birds and flowers that know nothing beyond the present moment – they do not farm or manufacture, and yet they eat and live successfully. He does not say don't **plan** for tomorrow, but he does say don't be **distracted** about tomorrow. The word "worry" in the text is translated from the Greek *merimnao* and could be literally translated "divided in mind" hence our English meaning of worried or distracted, where our mind is heading in different directions at the same time.

In contrast to consuming precious mental resources about what could possibly go wrong tomorrow, Jesus invites us to prioritise seeking after his kingdom today. His kingdom is where God is ruling right now. Getting distracted about the future means we miss what God is doing today. This is the root problem of all worry, fear and catastrophising - we create a fictional mental narrative of how and where life goes terribly wrong in the future. We can also be equally consumed by fantasies of a supposedly ideal future that will not happen – an equally fictional mental narrative. And these are fictions: the future does not exist; the present moment is our only genuine reality. The future is not your life – your life is right now.

---

[53] Matthew 6:25-34

BUT WHAT ABOUT MY GOALS?

Before leading you into overly-radical conclusions, I will say that there are times it is wise to think about the future. For example, you may have specific goals that you are working towards, and achieving goals takes planning and preparation. And when planning, it makes good sense to consider things that might not work out and prepare accordingly. This is known as risk management in the professional world, and it is prudent and sensible. However, all this planning and preparation can be done as intentional present-moment activity rather than unfocused distraction.

There is always a small danger to any future planning, and that is to allow the future to become more important than the present. For any goal you are working on, focus fully on the immediate task and invite God into it rather than constantly wishing away the present and the goal accomplished. There will just be another goal after that to distract you from the present. Do not focus on today's activities as a stepping-stone to something else. Recognise your life journey as an adventure, not just an obsessive need to arrive.

Paul's letter to the Colossians contains this challenging quotation:

> ...and in him you have been made complete, and He is the head over all rule and authority; [54]

It says we have been made complete in Christ. If we genuinely embed this in our thinking, it unloads all pressure from any future life goals we have. Recognising from God's perspective that there is nothing to add, our goals can be held far more lightly than if our

---

[54] Colossians 2:10

identity depends on them. You may well have goals to attain and things to acquire, but if on a deeper level you recognise that you are already complete, it removes the need for grim determination to *achieve* in order to become something. You also will not be held back by fear of failure if your true sense of self does not depend on your personal successes.

Many carry around a deep-seated sense of lack or incompleteness. For those aware of this feeling, it carries a sense of not being good enough; for those unaware, it translates into a constant craving for more: more things, more power, more money, more social status, more education, better relationships, and any other craving you can think of. All of these trying to prop up your identity. But when we are brave enough to think towards the end of our short life, all these cravings diminish dramatically in importance. Frequently, those who have had a close brush with death through illness or accident discover a fresh perspective on what really matters.

In the same vein, many people never recognise there is no true fulfilment in anything they do or possess. Those that do open their eyes and recognise this, but who do not have a spiritual lens on life, will risk becoming nihilistic and despairing – what is the point in anything? The thoughtful person is right to despair about the lack of life-meaning without God. Ecclesiastes is the Bible's philosophical exploration of purpose and fulfilment. It covers the entire journey and after twelve chapters reaches a single conclusion:

> *After all this, there is only one thing to say: Have reverence for God, and obey his commands, because this is all that we were created for.* [55]

---

[55] Ecclesiastes 12:13 (GNB)

Nothing you see or do will last. In Paul's Corinthian letter we are reminded of the temporary nature of everything we can see:

> *So we fix our eyes not on what is seen, but on what is unseen, since what is seen is temporary, but what is unseen is eternal.* [56]

If you can see it – it won't last, keep that in mind for everything you plan and every goal you set. Eternal things are not visible to the naked eye and our genuine identity is in Christ whom we cannot see.

THE CONFLICT OF WAITING

Closely related to future distraction is the idea of waiting. We tend to encounter waiting in two forms – short term and longer term waiting. Short term waiting includes things like waiting your turn in a line, waiting in traffic, or waiting for a friend you are meeting. Longer term waiting might be things like waiting to get married, or waiting for a new job, or waiting for a hospital appointment. In all these cases, there is a natural tendency for us to wish away the present and for the future to hurry up and get here. Doing this we are throwing away a wonderful opportunity. Just think of the phrase "killing time", which equates to deliberately throwing away the opportunity of the present moment before us.

Any kind of waiting creates a level of conflict – it implies you want to be in the future rather than the present. Why not completely give up the idea of waiting, and embrace the moment now? At some level, whenever you consider yourself to be "waiting", you are not accepting the present. Like the slave we talked about before who is waiting to be freed, or the person

---

[56] 2 Corinthians 4:18

carrying the soldier's heavy pack, who is waiting for the job to be finished; does it have to be waiting, or can it be living in God's presence now?

That said, I find this a struggle. I hate to be kept waiting. I write these words as much for me as for anyone. When someone I am meeting shows up late and says: "sorry to have kept you waiting", I want to say: "Really? Are you really sorry? Was that the best you could do?". What if it never occurred to me to say that because I was too busy enjoying the presence of God now – rather than worrying when someone would show up. As I'm writing these words, I'm quarantined in the Covid-19 pandemic. It is so tempting to wish away the current time until everything is "normal" again, but that is a missed opportunity. Let us seek God now, because right now is the only time we have to make room for the presence of God.

DO WE TRULY UNDERSTAND PATIENCE?

What we think of as waiting, scripture talks about extensively under the heading of "patience". There are many references to the value of patience – here's an example:

Be still before the Lord and wait patiently for him; [57]

Perhaps one reason we struggle to receive encouragements about patience and choose to claim we are just not very good at it is that **we just don't get it**. We misunderstand patience, thinking that it is successfully putting up with the present in order to get to the future, rather than recognising that the problem is not with the present, but with us and our desire to get away from it. The above verse from Psalms links us being still before the Lord with

[57] Psalm 37: 7

waiting patiently. We are bringing the Lord into the present situation, not gritting our teeth until the future arrives.

"Waiting on the Lord" is not the restless waiting where you are wishing away the current situation and you simply see the present moment as an obstacle to what you want in the future. It is alert presence with no tension, no fear. Not problem-solving, daydreaming, remembering, or anticipating; simply alert presence.

IS YOUR MIND USING YOU?

"I think, therefore I am". [58]

Famously said by the French philosopher and mathematician Descartes. Although not exactly aligned with Descartes' strictly philosophical intent, it does reflect a common modern perception that we are no more than the sum of our thought processes. It is, however, a huge mistake to equate your thinking processes with your identity. As we have already seen looking at the past and the future, our thoughts often tell us unhelpful stories – and in the case of the future, entirely fictional ones. Modern psychotherapy such as ACT[59] echoes this encouragement to decouple our thoughts from our identity and subsequent behaviour, calling the process "defusion". For example, if you say something like "I am worried", is that *really* you? The narrative about being worried which your mind is telling you does not have to define who you are. With practice this mental narrative can be treated almost like a radio playing in the background – it is just noise, it is not who you are.

---

[58] From *Discourse on the Method* (1637) - later adapted as "I am, I exist" in *Meditations on First Philosophy* (1641) .
[59] Acceptance and Commitment Therapy – www.contextualscience.org/act

In one of his letters, the apostle Paul talks about our weapons not being worldly ones:

> *We demolish arguments and every pretension that sets itself up against the knowledge of God* [60]

Some may think this is talking about Christian apologetics, where we out-reason the other person about the existence of God, or the resurrection of Jesus. It is exactly the opposite: demolishing the reasonings that get in the way of us knowing God. As we have seen earlier looking at Job, human reason may help us learn about God, but it is not enough to help us get to know him personally.

A great way to demolish things is to take out the foundation, and one foundation stone to remove is realising that we don't need to believe the lies our heads often tell us: about the past – that we should hang on to our regret, disappointments, resentments and guilt; or about the future – that we should take seriously our fears, anxieties and fantasies. If we demolish all this unhelpful reasoning, it makes space for us to be still and know God.

---

[60] 2 Corinthians 10:5

STUDY AND DISCUSSION QUESTIONS

1. How much of your identity is tied up in the past? What is good and bad about this?

2. Where have you found looking back to be helpful and unhelpful?

3. Do you notice your mind telling you unhelpful stories? How have you dealt with it?

4. What is your biggest struggle with the future - anxiety? fantasy? something else? What could you do about this?

5. Have you noticed yourself killing time? What other options are available?

The Present Moment

Exercise VIII. EMBRACE THE PRESENT MOMENT

This is a good exercise for which to put both plans and prompts in place. It is a very short exercise and can be done often. Become intensely conscious of the present moment as a gift from God, create space where you are highly alert but not distracted by thinking – put all your attention on the singular task you are doing now rather than letting your attention drift to something else. Decide you want to be where you are now, not somewhere else. Take everyday things and make them an end in themselves rather than only a means to something else, such as washing hands or walking upstairs.

Notice what past or future distractions your mind puts in front of you and instead choose to be actively present with God now – like the lily, like the bird.

Check that you are not feeling stressed and check if there is joy and ease in what you are doing, these are clear indicators if you are embracing the present or not.

Whatever you do, work at it with all your heart, as working for the Lord. [61]

You can plan by deliberately setting aside time before other activities to do this; and you can put prompts in place by using everyday activities such as sitting down as a reminder to be present.

Exercise IX. PLAY THE WAITING GAME

The game is this: if you catch yourself waiting then you have won the game.

Your reward for winning is the opportunity to stop waiting for the future, and to mindfully embrace the present moment.

You may be thinking of waiting in line, or waiting for a delivery, but there are also many smaller pauses in the day; pauses so small it is barely even worth reaching to check your phone. Why not use these pauses to take a deep breath and be still with the Lord?

Exercise X. SET DOWN HURTS FROM THE PAST

If you find yourself getting hooked up in negative emotions from the past, including resentment, unforgiveness, guilt and regret, then set time aside to deal with it. Toxic emotions hinder our approach to God; as Jesus said, if you are holding onto unforgiveness then sort it out before you come to worship.

Recognise that not all "difficult" feelings are toxic – grief and mourning are natural processes. Ecclesiastes tells us that there is a time to mourn and a time to dance. As we saw in the earlier

---

[61] Colossians 3:23

section on acceptance, Nehemiah came to God in mourning and God used it to initiate a great work.

For this type of exercise, it can be helpful to enlist a companion to support you and regularly check in with you. If you have deep seated trauma it is unlikely that following a written exercise alone will be sufficient and it would be unwise to attempt it without support and prayer. The exercise I describe is suitable for getting out of our own way to make room for God's presence and provide emotional "first aid", but it is no substitute for professional support where that is needed.

There are some key principles to bear in mind for this:

Do not go looking for problems. Certain strands of therapy relish in digging up past hurts to resolve them. I see nothing in scripture, my experience, or research that would support this. If the past is not causing you problems do not go looking for them.

Decide you want to put it down. At times, our past problems become part of our identity – "I am the wronged party" or "I always mess this up" or "I could never forgive this person". You need to be honest with yourself if you are ready and willing to move forward. It may be that you only have a willingness to be willing but are not quite feeling it yet – that is enough. If you genuinely are not willing to consider putting it down, you have probably stopped reading by now, but if you are still here, then take time to study, pray and seek wise counsel until you feel able to deal with it.

Recognise that some difficult feelings need to run their course. It is foolish to tell a grieving person that it's time to move on. Grief and mourning need to be processed, and there is no set time for this. Be patient with yourself and others.

If having considered the above, you feel ready, then follow part 2 of the exercise below – *Lean in deeper*. This practice is based on and expands the earlier *Lean In* exercise which you may have already tried out.

Exercise XI.   LEAN IN DEEPER

As you start, commit your time to God and ask for his grace. It is important to be aware of Bible truths about your situation but recognise this is the start of the process not the end. For example, suppose you were feeling guilty and said to yourself: "it says in the Bible my sins are forgiven so I don't need to hold onto this". You may win the reasoned argument but find the feeling is still there. That is OK.

Acknowledge the difficult feeling without judgement. Acknowledge your unwillingness to let it go if that is how you feel. There will be a temptation to start ruminating on the feeling and replaying all the reasons you feel that way. Rather than this, direct your attention from the outside-in and be the watcher, observing the feeling without analysing it or pushing it away. As you watch, be compassionate, show it unconditional love. Giving the feeling attention does not mean getting absorbed by it, but being the observer, the compassionate watcher. Acknowledge and accept it for what it is. Welcome God's presence around it.

In most cases you will be able to locate the feeling somewhere in your body. If you do, then turn your attention to that part of your body and carefully observe it, noting if it is a particular size or shape, or even colour. Then imagine surrounding it with love, warmth and light.

If you cannot locate the feeling in your body, imagine it as a crying baby that you are comforting. Offer kindness and compassion. As the pain starts to shift, thank God, and acknowledge his goodness and grace.

There is no set time to spend on this, or how many times you may need to repeat the process, only you will know that.

Exercise XII.   AVOID FUTURE FICTION

If you find yourself thinking about the future, then see if it is one of these:

- You are intentionally taking time to set goals, prepare or plan

- You are relaxing by thinking about something you have planned or would like to do

- You are fantasising about things that will never happen – daydreaming the hours away

- You are distracted by anxiety or fear

For the first two, please do not let me stand in your way! For the third, ask yourself if it is a good use of your time, this can be an unhelpful distraction. If it is the last, then according to Jesus, do not stand for it - anxiety and fear are worth the effort of dealing with. It is helpful to recognise from scripture that anxiety is not God's plan for us and according to Peter's letter you can: *Cast all your anxiety on him because he cares for you.* [62]

Firstly, check if you can simply set it down like the heavy bag we have talked about. Now it has been brought to your attention, that may well be an option. If the feeling is persistent however, then use the *Lean in deeper* exercise right above which we used

---

[62] 1 Peter 5:8

for setting down hurts from the past. You can also use the earlier *Embrace the present moment exercise* to good effect.

Whole books have been written on coping with anxiety and it can be a difficult habit pattern to break. It may well be that you will need more than this one short exercise to overcome, so do be patient and kind with yourself and seek additional help as needed. I also suggest returning to the section on Unconditional Acceptance and spend time pondering Paul's secret, thoroughly internalising this idea can be transformational.

CHAPTER 8

Not only when, but where

When people talk about encountering the presence of God, at times they associate it with a physical place. If a place becomes known as somewhere where a lot of people meet God, some people, especially those with a Celtic Christian background call it a "thin place". Thin, because the gap between heaven and earth seems thinner than usual.

Here in the UK, I greatly enjoy spending time on the Holy Island of Lindisfarne where Christian monks first established a place of worship in the 7th century. On the island itself, there are "prayer holes" on the southern cliff face which St. Cuthbert was said to have used as a place of quiet prayer – perhaps this might qualify as an extra-special place. Many readers may think of other similar locations, or retreat centres in this way. These are usually places where there has been sustained prayer and worship offered over many years. I have sat in the prayer holes on Holy Island and it does feel special. We have already talked about God's presence being in the here and now, wherever and whenever that is, but should we simply dismiss special places, or do they have something to offer us?

THIN PLACES IN THE BIBLE

The Old Testament has many narratives of God meeting his people in a physical location:

When Moses met with God speaking from a burning bush, God said: *"Take off your sandals, for the place where you are standing is holy ground".*[63]

When Jacob was in the wilderness and God speaks to him in a dream (it's the well-known one with a ladder) he wakes up and says: *"Surely the LORD is in this place, and I was not aware of it."* [64]. He describes the place as the house of God and the gate of heaven and names it Bethel - Hebrew for "house of God".

Moses had a special tent to meet God in – Exodus describes this:

> *Now Moses used to take a tent and pitch it outside the camp some distance away, calling it the "tent of meeting...*
>
> *...whenever Moses went out to the tent, all the people rose and stood at the entrances to their tents, watching Moses until he entered the tent. As Moses went into the tent, the pillar of cloud would come down and stay at the entrance, while the Lord spoke with Moses..* [65]

Also in Exodus, a tent of meeting was made as a physical "court of the Lord" which was for all of the children of Israel – the Tabernacle. God describes the Tabernacle as "a sanctuary for me" where "I will dwell among them". Generations later when the Israelites had settled in the promised land; King Solomon built a temple. In both the Tabernacle and the Temple, God made himself known in striking ways with cloud and fire.

---

[63] Exodus 3:5
[64] Genesis 28:16
[65] Exodus 33:7-11

So, there is clear evidence in the Bible that some places were out of the ordinary for meeting with God but that's not the whole story. Some of these places were mobile (like the tents) and all of them were temporary. Take the solid, well-crafted temple for example: the Israelites built three of them over the historical timeline of the Bible and each was subsequently destroyed by invading armies. Perhaps there are difficulties getting too attached to particular places for finding God's presence.

Jesus illustrated this point when talking to a Samaritan woman. The conversation had moved around to places of worship, and she raised a hot theological topic of the day: Where was the best place to worship God? Mt Gerizim or the temple in Jerusalem. The narrative is recorded in John's gospel, and as was Jesus' habit, he took the conversation to a whole new level:

> *Woman, believe me, the hour is coming when you will worship the Father neither on this mountain nor in Jerusalem. You worship what you do not know; we worship what we know, for salvation is from the Jews. But the hour is coming, and is now here, when the true worshipers will worship the Father in spirit and truth, for the Father seeks such as these to worship him. God is spirit, and those who worship him must worship in spirit and truth."* [66]

Jesus is quite clear – it is not about physical location. After the founding of the church, generations of Jesus' followers stood out from their religious contemporaries in the near-eastern world of the time by not having holy places. Christians met in homes or public spaces to pray and worship. As the church became part of the establishment in later centuries, buildings became important

---

[66] John 4:21-24

once again, but there is no indication in the Bible that they should be an essential part of meeting with God for his followers.

Is there therefore any benefit in seeking particular places for the presence of God? It's clear that God has used particular places for meeting with his people, but is not limited to them. Christian experience also suggests that at times there are places where his followers meet and worship which have a sense of spiritual momentum and expectation. I have served on youth camps where for the week of the camp there is a tangible sense of God's presence, extraordinary things happen, and it seems far easier to connect with God. There is a hard-to-beat example of this in the book of Acts:

> He took the disciples with him and had discussions daily in the lecture hall of Tyrannus. This went on for two years, so that all the Jews and Greeks who lived in the province of Asia heard the word of the Lord. God did extraordinary miracles through Paul, so that even handkerchiefs and aprons that had touched him were taken to the sick, and their illnesses were cured and the evil spirits left them. [67]

Paul comes to Ephesus, and with a group of about twelve believers starts a church that shares the good news of Jesus around the whole province and became a centre of miracles and healing. It was wonderful and special – but temporary, for the two years Paul was there.

My take-away from this is we can enjoy such opportunities as they arise, but not risk turning them into a crutch where we rely on them for connecting with God.

Continuing to think on place, Jesus had a regular practice emulated subsequently by the Christian desert fathers and

---

[67] Acts 19:9b-12

monastics of all generations: finding a place to carve out quiet time alone with God.

> *Very early in the morning, while it was still dark, Jesus got up, left the house and went off to a solitary place, where he prayed.* [68]

> *But Jesus Himself would often slip away to the wilderness and pray.* [69]

Here it is more about finding any suitable undisturbed location as opposed to a particularly hallowed place. Then using this for uninterrupted time to pray and exercise the stillness we have already explored.

THE ULTIMATE THIN PLACE

Having said that there does not seem evidence of an ultimate thin place in the Bible, let me now introduce you to one. The title of "ultimate thin place" comes from a comment made by a friend when I was teaching on this subject. As often happens with spiritual things, the thing we went off searching for was under our nose the entire time: that is ourselves. Us. Our body and mind.

In some church traditions, the body has had a rough deal over the centuries as a home of sinful actions where nothing good comes from. This has been a perennial issue in the Church, from the first century onwards, when the early church had to counter teachings of the Gnostic sect, who promoted everything physical as evil.

My challenge to us is that if we are looking for a physical dwelling place for God today where we can experience his

---

[68] Mark 1:35
[69] Luke 5:16

presence, we need look no further than ourselves. Scripture makes clear in many places that God lives in us. When Jesus is teaching and praying with his disciples shortly before his arrest, he says:

> "Anyone who loves me will obey my teaching. My Father will love them, and we will come to them and make our home with them. [70]

If we follow him, the Father and the Son will make their home in us. This is confirmed in Paul's letters. Such as the letter to the Colossians:

> ...the glorious riches of this mystery, which is Christ in you, the hope of glory. [71]

The first letter to the Corinthians:

> Do you not know that your body is a temple of the Holy Spirit, who is in you. [72]

The first letter to Timothy:

> Through the power of the Holy Spirit who lives within us, carefully guard the precious truth that has been entrusted to you. [73]

The "glorious riches" of God's secret is "Christ in us" says Paul. The Holy Spirit lives within us and we are a temple – a place where God lives and is worshipped.

So now the big question: is this some figurative language that means something other than it says? Perhaps God lives with us in some mystical way that does not include our body. Or does our God in truth live within us? Where possible, I always adopt the

---

[70] John 14:23
[71] Colossians 1:27b
[72] 1 Corinthians 6:19a
[73] 2 Timothy 1:14

straightforward interpretation of the scriptures I read, and I see no reason not to take these teachings at face value: We are the temple of the Holy Spirit – a place designed for the worship of God. Us. Our physical bodies. The scripture is clear, God dwells in us.

Yes, really.

Now the next big question: have you stopped to think about this? If we really believe this truth, it takes off the table trying to seek special places to connect with God.

This is true of the individual believer and also of the gathered church which Paul's Ephesian letter says *rises to become a holy temple in the Lord.* [74]

Returning to the Colossian letter:

Since, then, you have been raised with Christ, set your hearts on things above, where Christ is, seated at the right hand of God. [75]

Having been told it is "Christ in us", right here, down on earth, we are now told that we are "raised with him" and he is seated at the right hand of God. So, in some spiritual manner we are with Christ above, seated with the Father, and also he is down here with us! Starting to wrap our heads around that we are now encouraged to direct our inner world, our hearts, to the place where Jesus Christ and his Father are after being told we have been "raised with Christ".

So one way to direct our hearts on the things of God, is to **recognise his presence in us.** Why not turn our attention inward

---

[74] Ephesians 2:21
[75] Colossians 3:1

and remind ourselves that we are his temple and He has graciously made his home in us? Take our intentional attention and direct it throughout our body, recognising that it is Christ in us – and Christ fills *all in all* [76] as it says later in the same chapter.

Psychotherapists have long used techniques of "grounding" in the physical body to help people deal with panic attacks and other anxiety disorders. In these, you perform an exercise to systematically scan your attention across different parts of your body and focus on its very physicality.

It seems significant that as purely a mental exercise this can have a stilling effect on the mind. We have opportunity to undertake a similar practice, but with the added insight of our body being the temple of the Holy Spirit.

---

[76] Colossians 3:11

STUDY AND DISCUSSION QUESTIONS

1. Have you found special places helpful in your faith journey? What has made them so?

2. Can you relate to your physical body being the temple of the Holy Spirit, somewhere where God lives? What makes this easy or difficult?

3. Can you relate to the entire Christian church being the temple of the Holy Spirit? What does that mean in practice?

4. What are your experiences of taking sustained attention into your body?

PRACTICAL PAUSE

Place

Exercise XIII. FINDING A SPECIAL PLACE

Having determined that special places are not essential to finding God's presence, many find them helpful. Visiting places of pilgrimage by nature of the process: investing time, effort and money, and the anticipation of joining with others can be powerful catalysts.

On a more mundane note, regularly finding quiet space to connect with God is exactly what Jesus did. There is a benefit in repeatedly using the same place. Your brain will tend to form an association of the place with devotional time, and it is likely you will be able to move more effectively into your devotional practice. What will be your regular special place?

Exercise XIV. RECOGNISE CHRIST IN YOU

Take time to turn your attention to your physical body. This is very much like the *Simple Stillness* exercise taking your attention into your body rather than specifically focusing on your breathing.

Consider the truth that it is Christ in you and let your mind dwell on that, as you give attention to your body.

You can do this as an extended quiet exercise. You can also do it with promptings through the day. Reminding yourself that it is Christ's hands behind your hands as you serve those around you. Reminding yourself that it is Christ's mouth behind your mouth as you speak words of encouragement and love.

If when you apply attention to the body, it brings up emotional pain and discomfort, it's likely bringing to light something that was there already, and if you're able, focus your attention and compassion on it, having in the back of your mind that it is Christ, the healer in you. If it at all starts to become overwhelming – you have flashbacks or sense an escalation of panic, then stop immediately. It is likely you have some deep unresolved trauma that you may need to seek professional support to resolve.

The temptation may be to ignore or suppress the feeling. If you do this, it will not go away, but simply be pushed down and remain a continued source of unease that can readily get in the way of welcoming the presence of God. Take a look at the *Lean in deeper* exercise for more detail.

CHAPTER 9

The right response in any situation

L et us consider the invitation of Psalm 100:

> *Enter his gates with thanksgiving and his courts with praise;* [77]

Here is a clearly outlined pathway into the courts of the Lord – thanksgiving and praise. In some ways it seems the opposite of the stillness we have already discussed, and yet these are two different ways we are being intentional with our attention to God. Most of us will find ourselves more comfortable with one or the other, yet why not embrace both? There is a thread of praise and thanksgiving throughout scripture:

> *I will give thanks to the Lord because of his righteousness;*
> *I will sing the praises of the name of the Lord Most High.* [78]

> *With praise and thanksgiving they sang to the Lord:* [79]

---

[77] Psalm 100:4
[78] Psalm 7:17
[79] Ezra 3:11a

I will give you thanks in the great assembly; among the throngs I will praise you. [80]

And as we shall see, while embracing praise, we cannot ignore lament, as so often the two are connected in scripture: in almost a third of the Psalms, the writer cries out to God in lament as well as praise.

PRAISE

In common language, praise is expressing approval or admiration. In a spiritual context, it is our response, our positive reaction to God for who he is or what he has done. It is doubtless easier to praise when you feel like it, but in scripture it comes across as a decision of will – no matter the circumstances.

Songs are probably the best-known form of praise, both in the Bible and in modern Christian practice. The Psalms were undoubtedly sung as written, but even within the Psalms, we are encouraged many times to sing a "new song" [81] – it seems that variety and mixing up old and new are very much encouraged. There is plenty of evidence that loudness is also encouraged, as is making noise in other forms like shouting and clapping.

Clap your hands, all you nations; shout to God with cries of joy. [82]

Throughout the Psalms we see musical instruments accompanying the people's praise, but beyond this, the very final Psalm shows us that the instruments themselves can be vehicles of praise.

---

[80] Psalm 35:18
[81] Psalm 33:3, 40:3, 96:1, 98:1, 144:9
[82] Psalm 47:1

Praise him with the sounding of the trumpet,
  praise him with the harp and lyre,
praise him with timbrel and dancing,
  praise him with the strings and pipe,
praise him with the clash of cymbals,
  praise him with resounding cymbals. [83]

And there's more: the above quote drops in dancing as a way of praising, as do other Psalms.[84] Lifting up hands is also a common one – do notice that it's commonly the *act of lifting* rather than hands being raised that is the act of praise:

Lift up your hands in the sanctuary and praise the Lord.[85]

Praise is not some formulaic, one-size-fits-all activity, it is exuberantly responding to God with sound and movement in almost endless ways: singing old songs and new, shouting, clapping, waving, dancing, playing instruments... It is an authentic, no-holds-barred expression which can be difficult for the reserved British among us.

In my younger days, although thinking I knew my Bible, I clearly had not appreciated this subtlety, let me explain. I was church-surfing and found myself towards the back of a church worship service one Sunday afternoon. It was a large room with lots of people, and there was a lot of singing, shouting, and moving around going on. I was not impressed. This did not fall into any of my comfortable categories of Things That Should Be Allowed In Church. I quietly endured, and when the pastor rose to speak, he opened with this comment: "*There is someone here who is despising our worship...* (then a pregnant pause) *... Do not despise*

---

[83] Psalm 150:3-5
[84] For example, Psalm 29:6, 87:7, 149:3
[85] Psalm 134:2 and, for example, Psalm 28:2, 143:6,

what God has accepted". He might as well have slapped me round the head.

Especially when God's people are gathered, praise and thanksgiving are pervasive: reflecting back to God how good he is, and showing appreciation for it. It is a way into the presence of God, and an almost automatic response when you are there. When Jesus enters Jerusalem in triumph and the streets are lined with crowds praising, he tells the Pharisees that if the people were silent, the stones would have to cry out [86]

LAMENT

As we read through the book of Psalms, we are not only struck by the consistency of praise, but also on the quantity of lament. We see cries of pain covering a wide range of emotions – grief, regret, doubt, anger, loneliness, confusion. We see the overwhelm of chaos, brokenness, and suffering. The frequency with which the Bible addresses this reminds us that this is a common and unavoidable human experience.

Earlier we looked at complaining, and biblical lament is different to the grumbling and complaining we read about in the Philippian letter. Lament is taking things we want to complain about and choosing to take them directly to God. Mark Vroegop[87], a theological specialist on lament says this:

Laments turn toward God when sorrow tempts you to run from him.

Almost a third of the 150 Psalms include an element of lament – look at these excerpts from Psalm 6: [88]

---

[86] Luke 19:40
[87] Mark Vroegop - author of Dark Clouds, Deep Mercy: Discovering the Grace of Lament
[88] Psalm 6:3,6 then 9

My soul is in deep anguish. How long, Lord, how long?

I am worn out from my groaning. All night long I flood my bed with weeping and drench my couch with tears.

Or Psalm 13: [89]

How long, Lord? Will you forget me forever? How long will you hide your face from me?

How long must I wrestle with my thoughts and day after day have sorrow in my heart?

We often see in Psalms like these that there is not only a narrative of difficult situations and emotions, but a feeling of abandonment by everyone, including God. Perhaps something we struggle to do, but the writers in the Bible were prepared to express the depth of their pain, doubt, and distress, even if it seemed somehow unspiritual or improper.

This is not the end of the story however - a consistent theme of the lamenting process in the Bible is moving through this and daring to trust God and turning to praise, rather than despair. So although lament feels the opposite of praise, the pathway of lament ends up on the doorstep of praise. Following the earlier cry, Psalm 6 later says this:

The Lord has heard my cry for mercy; the Lord accepts my prayer.

And Psalm 13 ends with this:

But I trust in your unfailing love; my heart rejoices in your salvation. I will sing the Lord's praise, for he has been good to me.

Thinking back to when we introduced the idea of acceptance – laments allow us to be real with our feelings, without pushing

---

[89] Psalm 13:1-2 then 5-6

them away. They are not resisting or denying what IS, but are our honest appraisal to God of what is going on in our heads and what we would like to see change.

THANKSGIVING

Closely related to praise is the idea of thanksgiving. It is hard to put an exact number on it, but there are over 100 encouragements to thankfulness in scripture. It is not just during times of corporate worship, but as part of a lifestyle. For example in Paul's Thessalonian letter:

> Rejoice always, pray continually, give thanks in all circumstances; for this is God's will for you in Christ Jesus. [90]

The phrases "always", "continually", "all circumstances" send a clear message which is to embed thanksgiving in our way of life so it becomes part of our individual personality and part of our church culture. We can confidently say that praise and thanksgiving are the right response in any situation.

At this point a question often arises: how can I be thankful for bad things happening? This is a misunderstanding of what is being said, there is no command to be thankful *specifically for* particular things in a situation which we perceive as bad. We are being asked to have a rejoicing and thankful attitude whilst we are in the situation.

As we explored earlier, we unconditionally accept the situation whatever it is, and now we have added to that an attitude of thankfulness to God. Take a look at the apostle Paul in the city

---

[90] 1 Thessalonians 5:16-18

of Philippi.[91] After preaching the good news of Jesus and healing a woman, he was beaten and thrown into prison with his friend Silas. At midnight they were praying and singing. Praising God whilst chained and in pain. I am confident that Paul's preference would have been a warm drink and a comfortable bed, but his circumstances were not a reason to stop praising God.

Praise, lament, and thanksgiving permeate the whole Bible, from the children of Israel, to the apostle Paul in prison, to the entire book of Psalms to Revelation. Let us make a practice of fully embracing them.

---

[91] Acts 16:16-40

STUDY AND DISCUSSION QUESTIONS

1. Do you find praise comes naturally or do you need to work at it? What about praise in difficult circumstances?

2. How broad is your experience of praise? What new things could you try out?

3. What are your experiences of lament?

4. What are your experiences of practising thanksgiving?

PRACTICAL PAUSE
Praise

There are endless ways to build praise and thanksgiving into our practice. Here are a few examples.

Exercise XV.   LITURGICAL INTENTIONALITY

Anyone taking part in a Christian church service will almost certainly have been invited to join in with congregational singing. If you do not like singing, there is a tendency to disengage, if you do like singing, the tendency is to get wrapped up in the music. My personal tendency is to theologically critique the words of the songs or complain about misspellings on the display.

As the purpose of the singing is for the group to join in praise to God, the challenge is to intentionally direct your attention onto the words as praise, and to consistently keep your attention there, rather than on what someone else is doing, or the shopping, or what's happening next. The same process applies to any liturgical act of worship you take part in, such as shared prayers or devotional readings.

Some will read this and say *Obviously! Of course!* This is written for the rest of us.

Exercise XVI. DEVOTIONAL PRAISE

Many frameworks for personal Christian devotions tend to focus on study and prayer, and less so on praise. As and when you set aside personal time with God, consider making time for praise. Working through the book of Psalms can be a valuable practice – picking one Psalm (or a portion of a longer one) and reading slowly and mindfully as if you were the writer can be powerful. The Psalms mix in the whole range of human emotions with praise to God and can be a wonderful way of linking however you are currently feeling into praise of God.

For a regular practice, Psalm 145 is a good choice. Known as the *ashrei* (with a few additions) – it is recited three times daily in traditional Jewish prayer. It is an acrostic Psalm, a literary device where each line starts with the successive letter of the alphabet. A Jewish commentator noted that *"the entire alphabet, the source of all words, is marshalled in praise of God"* [92]

Exercise XVII. LAMENTING WELL

When you are feeling the need to complain and recognise that there is a depth of feeling you cannot readily set down, it is time to lament. Lament typically goes through several phases:

Turning to God
Addressing the issue to God, rather than sitting on it yourself.

---

[92] Adelle Berlin – The Rhetoric of Psalm 145

Getting clear on the problem
Honestly identifying the pain, questions, and frustrations.

Dare to ask
Seeking God's help and asking specifically for what you need.

Trust and praise
Recognising God's trustworthiness and remembering the good things He has done.

These steps outline a common pattern seen in the Psalms of lament, and if this is your present need, it can be helpful to spend time reading and meditating on some of them. Here are a few that could be used: Psalms 6, 7, 10, 13, 38, 73, 130

Exercise XVIII. THANKFULNESS JOURNAL

There are so many encouragements to thankfulness in the Bible, we would do well to take the task seriously. One way to do this is a thankfulness journal.

- Start a journal with a series of prompts, or possibly different sections if you prefer, covering different aspects of your life: work, church, hobbies, home, relationships, for example.

- Under each heading, write down as many things as you can think of to be thankful for – past and present.

- Come back to the lists the next day and review them – add anything extra that you can think of.

- Do this regularly.

Exercise XIX. GRATITUDE PAUSE

Staying on the theme of thankfulness: create some prompts in your life, such as starting a new task, to pause and take a moment of appreciation and gratitude. It can be as simple as the fact you are still alive and able to do the task.

Another prompt for a gratitude pause is if you catch yourself complaining (one of our very first exercises). Do be aware though, that you are not trying to somehow balance out complaining with gratitude – seek to completely set down the complaining first. And do look at the *Lamenting Well* exercise.

CHAPTER 10

The best conversation you will ever have

It would be impossible for me to condense even a light touch of all the aspects of prayer into a single chapter and hence this section is not so much outlining a new pathway but drawing the book to a conclusion.

Firstly, what is prayer? Prayer at its essence is communication with God. Consider for a moment that:

- Communication is a two-way activity – talking and listening;
- Communication is best done in someone's presence.

The ground we have covered throughout this book naturally lends itself to communicating with God – becoming still and listening, focusing on the present, finding a good place, sharing praise and thankfulness. Anyone who has taken a listening skills course will tell you that a core part of listening is giving your attention to the one speaking. Focusing on what they have to say to you, and being open to their message, not jumping to conclusions. This sounds a lot like intentional attention and unconditional acceptance. Another listening skill is summarising what you've heard back to the other person, something we often do while meditating on God's Word.

So these different pathways cross again and again – stillness, the present, place, praise and prayer. And although this is not advertised as a book on prayer the practices therein are designed to enhance your life of prayer. Particularly when it comes to asking – for ourselves and others, something we have not covered, what better place to ask from than being at rest in his presence allowing us to *approach God's throne of grace with confidence, so that we may receive mercy and find grace to help us in our time of need.* [93]

As you continue your journey of faith, and explore different avenues of prayer, bring to your prayers your undivided, intentional attention, and be fully open to where God will take you with unconditional acceptance.

---

[93] Hebrews 4:16

STUDY AND DISCUSSION QUESTIONS

1. What do you find easy about prayer? And difficult?

2. Seeing that prayer is a mix of speaking and listening, what can help us find the right balance?

3. What routines could you develop to make your lifestyle more prayer-ful?

4. What styles of prayer do you make less use of that could be better incorporated into your lifestyle? (think: praise/thanksgiving, petition, confession, intercession – pre-written, extempore)

PRACTICAL PAUSE
Prayer

Virtually all the exercises in the book can be regarded as prayer in themselves or form part of your prayer life. Here are a few further examples building on the ground we have already covered.

Exercise XX.   PUPPIES TO PRAYERS

Our very first exercise was called "Check in on the puppy" where we deliberately pause to check in on what we are thinking. As part of this, errant thoughts or anxieties might become visible. We can set these aside as part of an acceptance process, we may also turn them around into prayers as Paul's Philippian letter encourages us:

> *Do not be anxious about anything, but in every situation, by prayer and petition, with thanksgiving, present your requests to God. And the peace of God, which transcends*

all understanding, will guard your hearts and your minds in Christ Jesus. [94]

If you spot a difficult thought, turn it into a specific request to God, covered with thanksgiving.

Exercise XXI. SPEAKING IN TONGUES

As a Christian you may speak in tongues. 1 Corinthians 14 describes this as praying privately to God in a way where the mind is not occupied. Since your mind isn't occupied, you may find it helpful to combine the *Simple stillness* or *Creation appreciation* exercises with speaking in tongues.

Exercise XXII. PRAYING FOR CHANGE

While looking at acceptance, we spent considerable time looking at difficult situations and noted that they may not be amenable to change, at least not immediately. This does not mean we cannot or should not pray for change if we believe it right to do so. However, by praying for change in a mindset where you are not resisting the current circumstances, you can pray from a place of peace and rest in his presence.

Circumstances may change following prayer – as when we looked at Nehemiah's pioneering work; or they may not: take for example Paul's "thorn in the flesh" [95] where he persistently prayed for the situation to change until God showed him that it would not. When we have unconditionally accepted what IS right now, we can pray confidently and not be wedded to outcomes aligned to our personal preferences.

---

[94] Philippians 4:6-7
[95] 2 Corinthians 12:8

Exercise XXIII.   REFLECTING ON THE LORD'S PRAYER

For our concluding exercise, let us look at the Lord's prayer. When Jesus' disciples said *teach us to pray*, this is what he taught them:[96]

> *Our Father in heaven, hallowed be your name,*
>
> *your kingdom come, your will be done, on earth as it is in heaven.*
>
> *Give us today our daily bread.*
>
> *And forgive us our debts, as we also have forgiven our debtors.*
>
> *And lead us not into temptation, but deliver us from the evil one.*

Choosing to meditate on and pray this prayer brings us directly into praise, trust and seeking God's will, taking us beyond ourselves into the loving arms of our heavenly Father. Here are some reflections to consider as you ponder this ancient prayer:

- What does God as "father" mean to you?
- How do you make his name holy?
- Where would you see God's reign coming closer?
- What is needful *today*?
- Where is forgiveness needed?
- Where do you and your neighbours need protection and support?

_____

[96] Matthew 6:9b-13

Afterword

Congratulations on making it to the end. If you have merely *read*, and not *done* - please take the time to explore the various practical exercises rather than treat this as an intellectual pursuit. Some of the exercises may have seemed strange or difficult but do not let that put you off.

Some things that sound simple are not easy - for example, our mind just keeps wandering when we try and be still no matter how hard we try. The temptation is to give up after a few tries but let me strongly encourage you to keep going. This is a common problem: the practices I cover are unfamiliar to most of us and it will take time to see change. Friends of mine have used a phone app: *Couch to 5k*, to start running regularly. For an experienced runner, 5k may be nothing, but for a beginner it can be a difficult mountain to climb. The running plan app takes 9 *weeks* to get to 5k by gradually building up the amount of running done and putting appropriate rest points in. We should not be surprised to need an extended period of time to see change when exercising our mind as well as our body. Just like keeping fit, making room for God's presence is a lifetime's work and if we want to see transformation, we will need to consistently take time to develop our spiritual life-skills.

My earnest prayer is that you will have been able to use these pathways to make more room for God's presence in your life: using your incredibly valuable attention intentionally, and then unconditionally accepting whatever your attention is resting on. Remember that presence implies present: here and now is the only time and place we have for connecting with God, let us treat every precious moment wisely.

In closing, may I pray for you, dear reader:

> *We continually ask God to fill you with the knowledge of his will through all the wisdom and understanding that the Spirit gives, so that you may live a life worthy of the Lord and please him in every way: bearing fruit in every good work, growing in the knowledge of God*[97]

---

[97] Colossians 1:9b-11

INDEX

AUTHOR'S NOTE

Thank you for reading, this is my first book. I had never seen myself as an author but after brewing on the content for several years and recognising that concepts across both psychotherapy and mysticism connected with teachings of Jesus and other things I had read in the Bible, I felt almost compelled to share. I had the twin goals of helping Bible-believing Christians connect with spiritual practices they may have been uncertain about, and helping spiritual seekers connect with the Bible in a way that is fresh and relevant.

If this book has added value to your life, please consider leaving a review on Amazon® or whichever platform you purchased from. Reviews are a huge help to me and other potential readers. And please join in the discussion online at presenceofgodhome.com

Printed in Great Britain
by Amazon